SADDLE FITTING

*HOW TO SELECT THE RIGHT
SADDLE TO FIT YOU AND
YOUR HORSE.*

by

WILLIAM G. LANGDON, JR.

Drawings by WILLIAM G. LANGDON, JR.
Technical Editor CHIC LANGDON

Published by

LANGDON ENTERPRISES

P.O. Box 201, Colbert, Washington

SADDLE
FITTING

Copyright © 1997 by Langdon Enterprises

Author
William G. Langdon, Jr.

Technical Editor
Chic Langdon

Drawings by
William G. Langdon, Jr.

Published by

LANGDON ENTERPRISES
P.O. Box 201
Colbert, Washington 99005
USA

Library of Congress Catalog Card Number: 96-94587

ISBN 1-883714-07-9

CONTENTS

CONTENTS

PREFACE

Saddle fit for the horse and the rider is not the main issue at the point of sale today. The last thing purchasers think of is: does it fit the horse? They may sit in the saddle for comfort, but do not know what that saddle should contribute in the way of design. Manufacturers of trees and saddles do not provide 'saddle fit' as part of the product. It is up to the buyer to select the correct fitting saddle for the horse and themselves. They do not want to have the issue come up and wish it would go away. Stores and catalogs today are not providing a 'try-it-out-for-fit' before you buy service.

This book is meant to help the buyer with a step-by-step program for selecting a saddle that will fit the horse and useful tips on what the rider should look for in a proper seat. Let me caution you, saddle-fit is not easy, but why have a saddle hurt a horse when a little extended effort on our part can find the correct saddle.

Most saddles, today, do not fit because the bars are too flat. We have more horses suffering with sore backs than ever before. Blanket and pad manufacturers have jumped to the front trying to cure poor saddle fit with thicker and thicker blankets. It can't be done.

As stewards of our horse's welfare we are charged with the care and comfort of our horses - when it comes to saddle fit we are not doing a good job. This material will help you do a better job of saddling your horses with the correct fit.

INTRODUCTION

The most notable contribution this book makes to good saddle fit for horse and rider is the white-pad-saddle-fit. A detailed explanation is included in the text.

The white saddle pad fit is:

1. Place a white saddle pad on the horse's back that has been marked with carpenter's chalk.

2. Then put the saddle directly on over the pad.

3. Mount the horse and ride for 15 to 20 minutes.

4. Now read the chalk marks off the white pad (the characteristics of fit). Does the tree fit the horse's back?

Read the text for a detailed explanation on this method of fitting.

75% of a rider's ability starts with the saddle. A good saddle makes a good rider. A poor saddle makes a poor rider. This text explains what is a good saddle.

WESTERN SADDLE PARTS

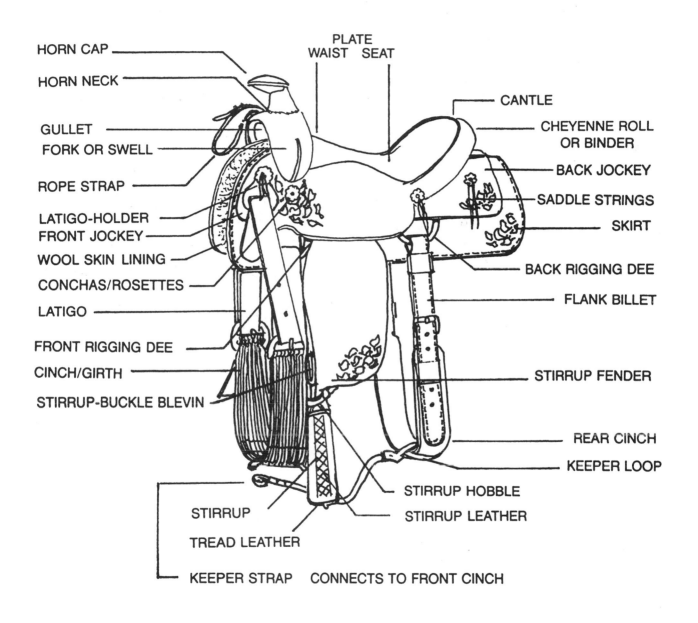

HORN CAP

HORN NECK

GULLET

FORK OR SWELL

ROPE STRAP

LATIGO-HOLDER
FRONT JOCKEY

WOOL SKIN LINING

CONCHAS/ROSETTES

LATIGO

FRONT RIGGING DEE

CINCH/GIRTH

STIRRUP-BUCKLE BLEVIN

PLATE
WAIST   SEAT

CANTLE

CHEYENNE ROLL
OR BINDER

BACK JOCKEY

SADDLE STRINGS

SKIRT

BACK RIGGING DEE

FLANK BILLET

STIRRUP FENDER

REAR CINCH

KEEPER LOOP

STIRRUP HOBBLE

STIRRUP LEATHER

STIRRUP

TREAD LEATHER

KEEPER STRAP   CONNECTS TO FRONT CINCH

ENGLISH SADDLE PARTS

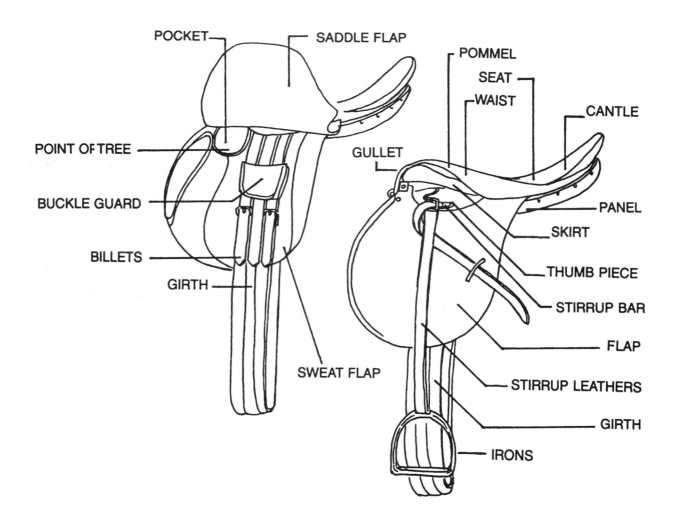

POCKET

SADDLE FLAP

POMMEL

SEAT

WAIST

CANTLE

POINT OF TREE

GULLET

BUCKLE GUARD

PANEL

SKIRT

BILLETS

THUMB PIECE

GIRTH

STIRRUP BAR

FLAP

STIRRUP LEATHERS

SWEAT FLAP

GIRTH

IRONS

GLOSSARY

TYPES OF SADDLES:	WESTERN SADDLES
PERFORMANCE SADDLE	Saddles used on performance horses (used in hard athletic uses/events) in contrast to pleasure horses.
PRE-50's SADDLE	Saddles built before the 1950's and before the California Equitation saddles became popular. Characterized by a forward seat in the middle of the saddle.
EQUITATION SADDLE	A deep seat saddle where the rider has contact against the cantle and the feet are forward. The rider's weight and seat are on the back of the saddle rather than in the middle. This does not allow the weight to be evenly distributed over the entire back.
A-FRAME OR SLICK FORK SADDLE	A-Frame saddle is an old style saddle that is higher in the forks and cantle than a slick fork saddle. The slick fork is a modern saddle with 8-1/2" fork and 4" or 5" cantle.
RECREATIONAL SADDLE	Saddles built for light use - often with plastic trees and lighter materials and construction techniques.
WORKING HORSE OR USING HORSE SADDLE	Saddles built for heavy use with bull hide or rawhide trees with stronger horns, materials and techniques.
	ENGLISH SADDLES
DRESSAGE SADDLE (training)	A forward seat saddle for classical riding. The saddle is characterized with center-seat, straight-down-flaps and high and wide panel. The stirrups are hung often just 2" or 3" ahead of the low spot in the saddle seat.
EVENTING SADDLE	A combination jumping and general purpose saddle for cross country, hunting and general riding. It has a combination seat. The seat and billets are back and the flaps are shorter. The stirrups are farther forward.
JUMPING SADDLE	Same as deep seat saddle, but even more pronounced change in the placement of the stirrups (farther forward) and the seat (farther back). The billets are standard. Built to free-up the front end of the horse in the take-off phase and then move forward over the neck during the vault to free up the back end.
CLOSE CONTACT SADDLE	The panel or under padding is thinner, especially in the throat/gullet, to effect a closer fit to the back. Often called a collegiate saddle in some marketing.

GLOSSARY

WESTERN TREES

Try the tree on your horse's back before you buy. Find a saddlemaker with blank trees to help you select a fit for your horse.

Trees will only fit certain styles of backs. Quarter Horse Horse on Quarter Horse, etc. They can be made to fit one horse, but generally they only come close to fitting very many horses backs. Each horse is different.

Each horse may need its own saddle. If you are lucky it may fit several horses.

ENGLISH TREES

Trees are available by seat length with only a slight variation in billet/girth placement.

The major styles of trees are: Modified Association, Cutter, Roper, Slick Fork, Old Slick Fork, Bowman, and Bronc. These are basic to being - slick fork or swell fork. They may be named after someone or they may be described in the name; such as a Will James, S.F. Bowman, Low Moose Roper, or Association. This is determined by the style of swells or forks and cantle you choose.

The bar widths and rafter angles come in: Full Quarter Horse, Quarter Horse, Semi-Quarter Horse, and Full Arab. This is determined by the style of back you order for your saddle.

In addition, you can order the cantle height, the length of the seat, the type of horn, the slope of the swells and the horn, the dish of the cantle, the width of the gullet and best of all, on custom saddles that are hand carved, the seat can be custom carved just for you. Narrow or wide or whatever.

The tree should be covered with rawhide (regular or heavy) and be laced with rawhide is best. Then it is shellacked to seal it. The tree is very strong, but not too flexible.

Trees come in spring trees, tube, and reinforced wood frame, depending on the manufacturer. The width of the seat bars is critical to avoid point loading onto the back. In addition, the tube types are not acceptable. The cheaper the saddle the less spring steel is in the gullet-bar. This needs to be flexible to 'work' with the expansion of the upper back behind the withers. Too stiff causes soreness.

Trees come in various gullet widths: some designated A, B, C, or D. Some designated: Extra Wide, Wide, Standard or Regular, or Narrow. These sizes are not standardized such that they are reduced to measurements between manufacturers.

Attachment of the stirrup hangers is also a critical feature of the integrity of the tree.

Saddle fit for the horse is a well accepted principle with English saddlers, but not always observed. The seat is available in deep, eventing, dressage, jumping, and combination. Most common are combination or all-purpose saddles.

GLOSSARY

GENERAL TERMS:	WESTERN/ENGLISH
PLEASURE SADDLE ALL PURPOSE SADDLE	A saddle that has a wide variety of uses. Examples are: Western - Flat seat roper's saddle, English - Eventing. Some pleasure saddles may be padded.
THE SADDLE FORMULA	A saddle that lets you ride balanced over the horse's center of gravity. A center seat.
STAND UP SEAT	A balanced seat over the horse's center of gravity with the rider's legs under the rider's weight. The same posture as if standing on the ground with your legs spread apart like you are riding. A line can be drawn through the back of the heel, through the hip bone and through the shoulder. The legs are not as far back as the dressage seat. This gives the rider more protection for faster, harder riding.
FLAT SEAT	The top of the saddle (plate) is flat from front to back.
EQUITATION OR CHAIR SEAT	Sitting on your 'cheeks' or pockets on the back of the saddle with your feet and legs forward, like sitting in a chair, makes the rider bounce and out of balance on the horse's back. It is hard on the horse's back and very hard to develop a good, quiet set of hands.
HIGH CROWN OR 'TILT-UP' SEAT. THE SLOPE.	The seat, or 'plate' or 'crown', tilts up to the front of the saddle and holds the rider in the seat-pocket. Limits the rider from moving forward or back. Low tilt-up seats are workable with rough stock riding and fast rough country riding. The seat-pocket is still in the middle of the saddle.
CUPPED CANTLE	The cantle has a concave seat versus a flat seat. Easier to stay on rough stock.
PADDED SEAT	Seat is padded for comfort.
CHEYENNE ROLL	A ridge or roll on the back of the cantle of a Western saddle.
SKIRTS	The large leather pieces that are under the bottom of the saddle, between the saddle tree and the horse. The pieces where the sheepskin is sewn on.
FENDERS	The leather on the stirrup leathers to protect the calf of the rider's leg.

GLOSSARY

STIRRUPS LEATHERS	The leather strips on a saddle that hold the stirrups. On a Western saddle they go over the bars; on an English saddle they go over the stirrup hangers.
SEAT POCKET	The lowest point on the plate for the rider to sit. Ideally, for good riding and proper fit, so the saddle is comfortable to the horse's back, it is placed in the middle of the saddle.
CROWN OR CREST	The narrow area on the plate ahead of the seat pocket.
WAIST	That portion of the Crown and the corresponding parts of the saddle where the legs fall over the saddle. These areas can be excessively thick or narrowed by the way the saddle is constructed. The saddle is more comfortable when narrower.
TWIST	A term to describe the 'bars' conformation from front to back on the saddle. The bars are twisted as they connect to the swells and flatten out under the cantle. A major problem area on English and Western saddles.
SWELLS/FORKS/POMMEL	The front of the saddle that is connected to the bars.
THROAT/TUNNEL/GULLET	The opening under the swells or pommel that fits over the withers and runs the length of the back. Should provide air flow to cool the back.
JOCKEYS/REAR HOUSING	Short skirts over the main skirts of a Western saddle.
SEAT JOCKEY	The leather that covers the seat area and partially under the rider's upper thigh.
HORN CAP	Leather cap over top of horn.
HORN COVER	Leather cover over and around the post of the horn.
HORN WRAP	Rubber, rawhide, or mule hide wrapped around the horn clockwise or counter clockwise depending on right handed or left handed cowboy to give traction to a rope when dallied around the horn.
SADDLE DEES	The brass or stainless steel rings or 'D' shaped rings for the attachment of the cinch or latigos or tugs on a Western saddle. Called the rigging.
BILLET	The 2 or 3 straps on an English saddle for attachment of the girth.

GLOSSARY

GULLET PLATE POINTS The end of the metal gullet plate (usually a 1-1/2" wide spring steel metal strap in the pommel of an English saddle) that ends below the withers pockets on the side of the horse. These are the source of much soreness.

PANEL The heavy pad under an English saddle that runs along the gullet and up under the cantle. This should be about 6" to 7" wide on either side under the cantle for an adult rider.

FLAPS That portion on an English saddle that goes under the legs to protect them from sweat and saddle fittings. These vary depending on the saddle style from straight down to well forward.

POMMEL The front portion of an English saddle compared to the swells on a Western saddle.

CANTLE That portion of a Western or English saddle that sticks up and forms the back of the saddle.

STIRRUP HANGER Metal hangers, on an English saddle, that the stirrups 'hang over' and are mounted on the gullet bar. They may be spring loaded or a low curve for the stirrups to 'pull off' in case of an emergency. With a Western saddle the stirrups go over the bars and do not come off.

WORKING SADDLE A rancher, trainer, or contestant saddle; very durable.

STOCK SADDLE An Australian or American rancher saddle.

ROPER SADDLE A roping saddle with double rigging, dally horn, flat seat and stand-up stirrups.

BUCKING ROLLS Used on an A-frame or Slick-fork saddle as a means to keep the rider from getting bucked off. This consists of two half-moon pads attached to the swells in front of the rider's thighs.

ROPE KEEPER A buckled or cut strap for tying the lariat rope to the saddle.

LATIGOS The strap used to connect the cinch, on a Western saddle, on the near side.

HALF BREEDS OR OFF BILLETS The strap on the off side to connect the cinch to the rigging. This is adjustable.

GLOSSARY

REAR CINCH

The second or rear cinch on a double rigging keeps the saddle from tipping forward. This is connected in front with a keeper strap to the front cinch. This keeps it from working back where the horse might get a foot through it in case of a fall.

CUSTOM SADDLE

Handmade to order saddle. Generally provided by a saddlemaker rather from a mail order or factory supplier.

CARVED SEAT

Over a metal plate called the 'strainer plate' tacked to the bars and cantle forming the seat is stretched several layers of leather. This is then carved to fit the rider and form the seat of the saddle.

RIGGING

The heavy leather straps or tugs that hold the latigos, half breeds, and cinchas. The rigging is fixed to the tree.

ROCKER

The curve along the bottom of the bars or panels, from the front to the back, so it will fit down into the low spot on the horse's back behind the withers. The curve of the bars fits the curve of the back.

RAFTER

The angle that the bars slope - like the rafters of a house.

SCAPULA HOOK

A piece of cartilage that sits atop the scapula bone in the horse's shoulder. The hook sits on the backside where it overhangs the scapula bone. Four major muscle groups connect/converge over this point. Thus, the saddle should be placed 2" behind this location. You can feel it with your fingers as a hard knot.

THE CURVE IN THE LAST RIB

Beyond the last rib on the horse's back there is little to support the saddle. Thus, the saddle bars or panels should not extend farther back than the curve of the last rib. This is about 7" or 8" from the ridge of the backbone.

1 PIECE SKIRTS

Skirts are all one piece. However, some less expensive saddles use several pieces to save leather costs. The overlap will cause soreness on the horse's back and is totally unacceptable in any case.

WAXED THREAD

Custom saddles have waxed thread, which lasts longer against moisture, and the thread lies in a groove, from the stitching machine, that you don't find on catalog saddles.

GLOSSARY

FLARE
The twist of the saddle bars comparing the front under the swells to the back under the cantle. Interchangable with twist.

CUTTING HORSE BARS
The mid-portion of the bars are thinner to accommodate a better ride. Makes a thinner waist.

WESTERN SWELLS
Determines the name of the saddle. The front portion.

SWELLS
The front of a Western saddle; vary with full swells at 11" to 13" wide, undercut swells are 13" to 14" wide and slick fork swells average 8" to 10" wide.

CANTLE STYLES
Come in regular, comfort, and shovel. The comfort cantle is rather flat across the top. Cantles are measured by height, width, and dish.

SEAT
The seat is measured from in back of the horn, or top of the pommel in English, to the cantle.

GROUND SEAT
Over the bars, bar risers are placed to make a place for the stirrup leathers to go over the bars, and these should allow for the stirrup leathers to swing freely. Over this is placed a thin layer of leather called the strainer, next is placed the strainer plate (galvanized sheet metal), over this are added layers of leather for shaping the seat. This can be shaved and shaped to fit a center seat, a deep seat, or a seat high in the front.

BULL HIDE TREE COVER
Bull hide is heavier rawhide, not bull hide.

RALIDE
Plastic tree trade name. The seat cannot be styled to fit the rider, you get what comes from the factory.

RAWHIDE
The wood tree is covered with untanned leather and laced together with rawhide or nylon laces. Cheaper trees are covered with canvas or fiberglass.

CLICKERS
Machines that pre-cut leather parts for saddles.

LEATHER
It takes a full hide to make a Western saddle. Good or firm leather the fibers are closer together. On the top side the hair holes are also closer together. Flanky leather is softer. A hide should not have soft spots. Most of the good cuts come from the rump and backline. Softer or 'flanky' cuts come from the bottom of the sides.

GLOSSARY

LEATHER TEST

Bend the leather to see how firm it is. Notice if it cracks or is filled with oil. Examine the grainy side and it should act like your own skin, but firmer. Where it is weak, is because it lacks hard packed fibers or dense fibers. Lightweight leathers are used on those parts of the saddle that require lots of shaping.

WESTERN RIGGING

Rigging comes in single or double. Styles include: built on the tree, rigged in the skirt, and flat plate rigged.

BLOCKED SKIRTS

Heavy skirts are best in helping distribute the weight over the back. The bars should be 'set' into the skirts, called 'blocked skirts', to work best. Real woolskin is the best for lining as it cools the back the best.

HORN FEATURES

The horn comes in different styles. It should have a spacer sewn in between the cap cover and the stem of the horn which indicates the cap cover will not slip loose in the future.

SEATS

Many padded seats have 2 pieces of leather over the cantle and seat to cut costs. The padded seat is to cover up this technique. Deep seats (on the back of the bars) are called Equitation Saddles: are built mostly for showing. Ranch saddles, training saddles, working saddles, and roping saddles are generally 'center seat' saddles, built to evenly distribute the rider's weight over the bars.

PADDED SEATS

Padded seats are good for recreational riding, but are not good for all-weather riding. Once they get wet they will likely make you very sore.

FLANK CINCH AND FLANK BILLETS

The flank cinch buckles into the flank billets or tugs.

SADDLE STRING

It is best to buy saddles where the saddle strings go through the tree and through the skirts. Cheaper methods just staple the skirts on and the saddle does not have the 'strength' as with strings.

STIRRUP ROLLER

The metal bar on top of the stirrup. Check the leather on the stirrup leathers at this point to be sure it is not cracked or worn.

HOBBLE STRAP

Holds the stirrup leathers together above the stirrup.

GLOSSARY

CINCH DEES	Cinch dees that are below the skirts keep the 'bulk' out from under the leg.
LEATHER RIGGING STRAPS	Leather rigging straps or nylon backed leather rigging straps at 2" width work well.
OFF BREEDS OR OFF SIDE LATIGO	Best in latigo tanned leather or nylon backed.
BUFFED LEATHERS	Buffed leather is done to make the leather seem smooth and remove imperfections. What is does is remove some of the grain side and this makes it weak - removing the strongest part of the leather.
SKIRT WOOL	If the wool backing is real leather then it is real sheepskin. Synthetic is not as good.
SKIRTING	Nothing should touch the spine and the skirts should not be sewn or laced together in back.
SEAT SIZES	Typically, 14", 14-1/2", 15", 15-1/2", 16", 16-1/2". Generally, measured from the base of the horn to the center top edge of the cantle.
ENGLISH GULLET SIZES	27 cm to 29 cm Very high withers 29-1/2 cm to 31 cm Average to high withers 31-1/2 cm to 32-1/2 cm Low or rounded back 32-1/2 cm Extra wide
STITCHED DOWN SEAT	Stitching in seat and cantle areas making the material look quilted or pleated.
TWIST - THE WORD HAS TWO APPLICATIONS	An application to English saddles means the narrow portion just ahead of the seat area and over the panels. With Western saddles it means the twist of the bars from front to back.
ONE POSITION SEAT	Saddles with a deep pocket so the rider is kept in one position.
MULTIPLE POSITION HANGERS	Stirrup hangers on English saddles that allow the stirrup leathers to be hung forward or back.
LEGS UNDER POSITION	As in a dressage seat.
STAND UP SEAT	Old frontier seat. Stirrup line is 5" to 6" ahead of the rider's center line. Rider is in the middle of the saddle, which allows the horse to balance the rider.

GLOSSARY

ENGLISH TREES

The seat portion on most English saddles will 'give' a little based on the type of construction of the tree or seat frame. The critical item is the pommel bar in the head; its width and rafter and the 'flare' at the ends. These points must not 'dig-into' the shoulder and the bar should flex with the expanding shoulders.

TREE FAULTS WESTERN

On Western trees the most common fault is the bars are too flat...they do not have enough rocker. Secondly, they do not have the proper twist. This is because the majority of all bars are the same today, made out of 2" x 6" material to be cheaper.

ENGLISH PANELS

The English saddle has the advantage of being able to have additional 'panel pads' sewn on the bottom of the main panel to achieve a fit if the tree is large enough.

The panel is the padding between the saddle and the horse's back. They are almost always too small to get the weight per square inch down to tolerable levels for the adult rider. They are also many times too straight or need more rocker and often 'curve' up too fast under the cantle losing contact with the back. The stuffing is 'supposed' to be able to be re-positioned to accommodate for the different shapes of the back. This is difficult to do as no openings are available to reach the stuffing without cutting the leather. In addition, most of the material used for the padding does not lend itself to 'unpacking' once it has been 'packed'. I have found this very hard to do an acceptable job. There are good fitting saddles available that meet the saddling equation. I have given you some basics for fitting, you will have to do the searching, fitting, and trying.

SADDLE SLIPPING AND ROCKING

If the saddle, Western or English, rocks from one side to the other, the gullet is not fitting correctly. It is generally too wide. If the saddle is continually slipping back or crawling forward, the rocker or 'bow' on the bottom of the saddle is not correct or it is too wide in the gullet. If it is 'high centered' in the middle the saddle will rock up and down on both ends.

FRICTION STRESS

Where the saddle 'rubs' excessively will cause soreness. Under the front and rear portions of the saddle are primary locations. Around the cinch location is another - causing excess heat. Watch the 'lay' of the hair and surface moisture for clues to friction stress.

GLOSSARY

GULLET CHANNEL
WESTERN AND ENGLISH

The gullet channel is the space under the saddle that goes over the backbone. The vertebra are very sensitive and susceptible to injury from abrasion and slow to heal. The backbone needs lots of ventilation or cooling and is one of the hotest places on the back. (Watch the snow melt off the backbone while the rib areas stay covered). Saddle skirts/panels should clear the top and sides of the spine comfortably. The saddle skirts should not be sewn or laced together over the spine behind the cantle on Western saddles.

STIRRUP LEATHERS

Stirrup leathers on Western saddles go over the tree bars and are generally 3" wide. To some folks the two thicknesses of stirrup leathers, the stirrup fender, and a Blevins buckle over a rigging strap is going to be just too wide to be comfortable. Take note of this when selecting a saddle.

In addition, check that the tree has a groove in it for the leathers to recess into on the underside of the tree, or else the heavy edge of the stirrup leather on the flat surface of the tree bars will undoubtably cause soreness. Ask about this.

Besides this, check that the stirrups can swing freely forward and back without catching. This is important to good riding, especially if the horse rears, bucks, trips, falls, or you use your legs for training.

HAND CARVED SEATS

Custom saddles give you the option to having the seat hand carved to fit your dimensions. Catalog and factory saddles are most often flat across the seat. A good hand carved seat will be flat and wide under the seat bones and narrow and peaked-up just ahead of the seat. This makes for a firmer and more comfortable seat. When the seat is too wide it is uncomfortable and harder to ride. Something to consider.

CHOOSING A FORWARD
OR DEEP SEAT SADDLE
The horse can balance your weight better with the forward seat.

There has been a big debate over this issue for umpteen years. My theory is the front of the horse is made to lift the back of the horse so the hinds can swing under and forward. That is the basic motion and the hinds drive the horse forward and the fronts carry the weight like a wheel barrow. The farther you sit back, the more the horse has to work to lift you and the rear end before he can draw the hinds forward. I have tried both ways extensively and I have had better results in every way with the bareback or forward seat.

GLOSSARY

POOR CONTACT SADDLE

An ill-fitting saddle will result in the loss of communications between the rider and horse. If a saddle is hurting the horse, it is not going to pay attention to the rider's weight, legs, or seat bone cues.

THE SEAT LOCATION

The seat of the saddle should be over the low spot on the horse's back. Generally, just behind the withers, or often referred to as the bareback-seat-location. The back half of the seat is best nearly flat and the front half is very narrow. The seat bones sit on the back half and the crotch sits on the front half. The shaping of this seat shape and its location, forward over the low spot on the horse's back, or farther back in the 'chair seat', is the function of the saddlemaker.

FITTING PLASTIC TREES TO THE HORSE

Refitting a 'plastic tree' (Western) to the horse's back is difficult because it is hard to see under the tree to examine the fit. The ground seat, that is part of the tree, sits right over the bars so you cannot see the fit. The plastic bars can be rasped for shaping and leather can be glued onto the bottom of the bars.

FLEXIBLE WESTERN TREES

English spring trees are more flexible than Western trees. Unfortunately, wood and plastic trees do not 'flex' with the horse's motion. What gives the most are the soft muscles of the horse's back as they absorb the pressure, especially in situations like hard reining, up and down hills, or roping where the back swells, stretches, and contracts.

FLEXIBLE/ADJUSTABLE SADDLES

Contemporary saddles on the market with new design features and materials aimed at better saddle fit. Older models included an adjustable angle. One newer design includes a flexible-modified-ball joint that allows for some rafter and rocker flexing at the forks and cantle. This will allow the saddle to fit when the horse is in motion and the back is changing shape. Something worth watching.

TREE-LESS SADDLE

Basically, a semi-bareback pad with a flexible under structure and a cantle and swells. The concept of fitting most backs and while in motion appears possible, but can it be cinched good enough not to roll on the back? There is no gullet channel and no stirrup leathers, only nylon straps that swing from the knee rather than from the hip. It appears to be good for trail riding. I will need testing to better understand its workableness.

GLOSSARY

STIRRUP LEATHERS WESTERN

Because they take such hard abuse and can be dangerous do not accept anything less than quality leather 15 to 16 ounces and no less than 3" wide.

STIRRUP LEATHERS ENGLISH

Because the leathers wear on metal top and bottom, inspect them continually for cracks. A broken stirrup leather on an English saddle can be very serious. I would not accept anything less than 1-1/4" wide and opt for some of the new extra strong leathers available.

STIRRUPS WESTERN

Stirrups are generally made of wood covered with rawhide, leather, or metal. The roller should also be covered with leather to protect the stirrup leathers from wear. Stirrups come in a variety of styles: Bell Bottoms, Bronc, Contest, Roper, Extra Wide Roper, and Oxbow. Plastic used on stirrups seems too light for me and they are always flopping around instead of hanging down. Most stirrups have a wide tread to rest the ball of the foot on.

Avoid stirrups like metal that could be crushed around your foot in a fall. This could lead to a disaster if the horse gets up and you can't get your foot out of the stirrup.

CINCHAS/GIRTHS Western straps that attach to the cinch should be double or more thickness. Single strap rigging is not safe.

Cinchas and girths are measured from end to end. English girths should buckle onto the billets on the leg flaps. Cinchas should be measured from a spot 3" back from the elbow and approximately 3" up. They come in even numbers: 30, 32, 34, 36, etc. Get cinchas or girths that will not sweat up, get hard on the edges, and gall a horse up. This is especially true for the person who is riding a lot. Mohair seems to be the best rather than cotton, and well tallowed leather with round edges is best for English girths. The fleece or woolskin girth covers are really bad for this, unless they are washed constantly. In fact, it is wise to have several extra cinchas or girths so you can 'switch' every few days. This gives you an extra, so one can be in the 'wash' and one drying all the time.

The wider cinchas and girths spread out the pressure and seem to grip better than the narrower ones.

LATIGOS AND BILLETS

Latigos should be of good 'latigo leather' and 1-1/2" to 2" wide to stand the stress. Billets on English saddles should be of good quality leather and 1" or better wide.

GLOSSARY

PICKING STYLES AND THEIR USES FOR THE WESTERN RIDER

Saddles come in all styles these days: THE GENERAL PURPOSE or ALL AROUND SADDLE used mainly for ranching, training, packers, distance riding. BARREL RACER, CUTTING and PENNER used as the name implies. ROPERS for competitive arena roping. EQUITATION SADDLES, deep seat or chair seat saddles, used for showing and parades. ASSOCIATION SADDLES, a using saddle favored by many ranchers and modified for saddle bronc riding.

SEAT TYPES AND INTENDED USES

Includes: slope, angle, position, spread, leg and seat room.

Western saddles are available in: FLAT SEATS, CENTERED SEATS, and DEEP SEATS. The competitive saddles for barrel racing and cutting have a flat seat providing different seat positions for maximum performance of the horse. Centered seats are common to using, ranch, and some roping saddles. Deep seats, with the stirrups forward, are generally recreational saddles used for showing, parades and short rides.

TREE BARS OR SADDLE FRAME

Bars are meant to carry the weight of the rider on the top of the horse's ribs where it is generally flat. Also, the bars are basically designed to spread the weight imposed on it evenly over the back not to exceed 1.5 pounds per square inch of surface. Most saddles do not even come close to meeting this design requirement.

The rocker, the rafter, the twist, the length, and the shaping of the face are all design requirements of the bars.

BUYING

Generally order 1/2" larger seat and if selecting a padded seat go for 1" larger.

SKIRTS INSIGHTS

Good wool skirting is best on skirts. Synthetics are not as good. This is especially true in steep mountain country, riding hard in rough country, or roping heavy livestock. Thick leather skirts well 'blocked' into the skirt distribute the weight, thin skirts are not desirable.

Skirts come in a variety of shapes from: Small Round, Large Square, Modern Square, and Butterfly.

FENDERS

Fenders should taper to the top to allow for proper swing under the seat jockey so the rider can keep his balance.

BUYING OR GETTING A GOOD SADDLE

This book is dedicated to helping you select a good saddle.

Getting a correct saddle for you and your horse is more important than you may realize. There are some very important characteristics about saddles that you may not be aware of:

1) MOST SADDLES DO NOT FIT THE HORSE'S BACK PROPERLY

2) MANY SADDLES DO NOT SEAT THE RIDER CORRECTLY

3) 75% OF HOW YOU RIDE DEPENDS ON THE SADDLE

A good saddle makes your horse perform better and it makes you ride better. Read this book and it will help you develop a set of guidelines for selecting a proper saddle.

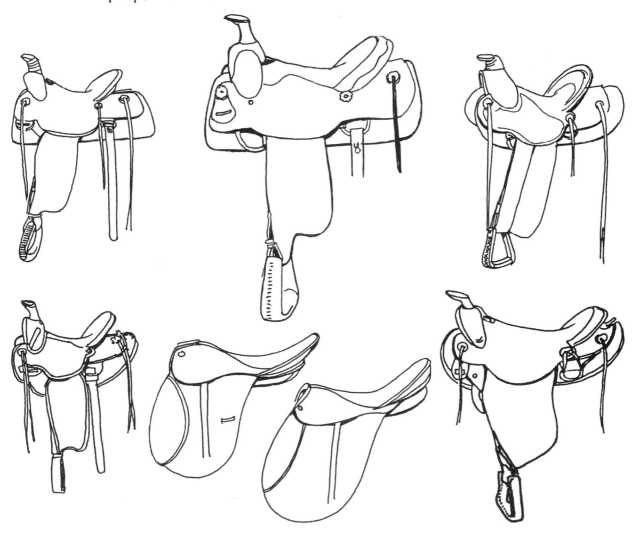

LEATHER

The best way to make a judgment on the quality of leather is to go to your local tack shop and inspect the leather in quality saddles and tack. Especially look at the English saddles or German saddles as a classic example. The leather has a gray like greasy feeling to the surface. When bent, it acts like your skin, it does not crack or separate, but wrinkles. It is very supple. Good leather lasts a long time and is very strong. Cheap leather is dry and the fibers show on the underside, it is weak and will break or tear under stress. It is not safe to use in stirrup leathers, reins, bridles or girths/cinchas. Good leather is pleasing to handle. Let your fingers have some time feeling good leather and they will tell you in the future which is good leather. It is not good quality if it is spongy, dry, stiff, or too soft.

Good leather saddles are easier to grip. Cheaper leathers are slicker and harder to ride. Those with a 'glossy' finish are slick; where good leather sort of 'clings' to you.

With good leather the hair holes are close together and on the underside the fibers are packed close together. Flanky leather is soft or spongy and the fibers are not tightly packed.

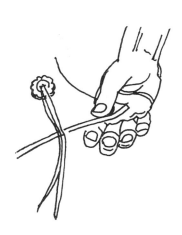

The best leathers always have come from slow maturing animals, like Aberdeen Angus, and from the colder climates where they do not get the warble holes in them. Old wire cuts are also bad. Oak bark has always been one of the best sources of tannic acid for tanning. Now, many chrome salts are also used, making a strong leather. Most leather in the U.S. is imported and of poor quality. Some European and U.S. companies still make good leather, a buyer has to be selective.

The way the leather is cut in half or full hide, butts or split, makes it different.

Colors maybe applied by the supplier or the saddlemaker. Favorite colors are: Light tan, light brown, rich brown, very dark and red latigo.

Oils added usually are cod oil or tallow.

Good leathers do not need to be as thick as cheaper leathers because they are stronger and last longer. Poor quality leather on halters, bridles and stirrup leathers is dangerous. Be selective, it is much safer.

CUTS AND TYPES OF LEATHER	SPLIT BOTTOM SHOULER HIP	LATIGO SKIRT ROUNDED	OAK TANNED PIGSKIN EMBOSSED	BELLY SLOW GROWTH HARNESS LEATHER

CHOOSING A STYLE OF SADDLE

I cannot select a saddle style for you - that you best do on your own. Study the different styles available for your activity. My recommendation is that you try different saddles first before making any choices. I would be more inclined to buy an 'all-purpose-saddle' rather than a specific saddle such as a 'cutting saddle' or a 'barrel saddle' because it limits your use rather sharply. Some of the 'flat seat' roper saddles with an average horn, and the stirrups a little farther back, (5" or 6" ahead of the center of the saddle) make very good 'all-purpose' Western saddles.

English saddles now on the market are <u>generally</u> - half for jumping and half for general riding - according to European manufacturers I interviewed - so they are considered deep seated. A good eventing saddle makes a good 'all-purpose' saddle with proper positioning for the rider. If your needs call for a specific style then try out different selections within that category.

An 'all-purpose' saddle would be generally more useful over the years than a specific-style saddle. Saddles last a long time if properly cared for - so my recommendation is - always get the 'general-purpose' saddle that has a broad range of uses. This also must take into consideration the other aspects in selecting a saddle that are brought out in this book.

ALL-PURPOSE SADDLES ARE BETTER FOR THE MONEY IN THE LONG RUN BECAUSE THEY WILL LAST LONGER THAN YOUR TENURE IN CERTAIN ACTIVITIES.

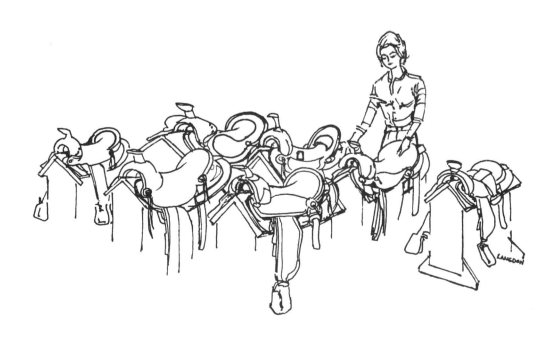

TYPES OF SADDLES

There are saddles today for every event in the horse world: cutters, penners, ropers, trail, ranching (in Western) and hunting, jumping, eventing, dressage, combined training, and general riding (in English) just to name a few ... and there are others. All specialty saddles!

Two major categories divide the English and Western saddle styles. In the English the divisions are: dressage seats and forward seats and all the others. In Western saddles it is working saddles and pleasure saddles.

The distinction in English saddles is the dressage seat has the exaggerated forward seat with straight down flaps and all the other styles have deeper seats and forward flaps.

With the Western the 'working saddle' is used by ropers, ranchers, trainers, and professionals. This is characterized, most generally, by a Stand-Up-Seat with the stirrups under the seat and a heavy rawhide cover over a wooden tree. All others do not meet this criteria.

THE EQUITATION FORMULA FOR SADDLES EQUALS A SADDLE THAT PUTS THE RIDER OVER THE CENTER OF GRAVITY OF THE HORSE. This means you are located forward over the Center of Gravity or Motion Center of the horse along with being able to ride in a 'Stand-Up-Seat and Over Your Legs'. Thus, your center of gravity is located over the horse's center of gravity and you can keep in this position at all the horse's gaits. Another way to say this is...

> THE SADDLE FORMULA IS A SADDLE THAT LETS YOU RIDE BALANCED
> OVER THE CENTER OF GRAVITY OR MOTION CENTER OF THE HORSE.

SADDLES AFFECT PERFORMANCE

If the saddle is hurting the horse's back - you are not going to get as much performance out of the horse. As the level of performance is increased - and as a rider gets better and demands more from a horse - the horse will not be willing to give you that extra motion or movement needed because of the pain or discomfort. They can handle it when doing the easy things, but as the motion increases so does the pain and the horse starts to resist your aids.

At first, the pain is tolerable for the horse - because horses take pain pretty well - but as time goes by that steady pain gets to be more than they can stand and things start to happen.

A comfortable back is central to a horse's performance. Fatigue and lameness are often the results. Other possibilities include trying to tell us that something is hurting. Caving in the back as we get on, or tripping or bucking are just a few paramount reactions taken by the horse.

Below are a few things to look for ....

. White spots or white hairs. Fall and Spring.
. Swellings
. Swaybacked and sore to the touch.
. Ripple like scars on the skin and ruffled looking hair.
. Cold backed. The back gets hard in anticipation of the saddle. May buck with rider's weight, or sink down when saddled. Some hump-up at first or when mounted.
. Act stiff at first or slow to get going.
. Acts real spooky when first mounted.
. Tripping and stumbling or catching a front or hind.
. Does not like to climb or go down hills and often turns up sideways going down hills, or does not travel straight on the flat.
. May not like to be brushed.
. Trying to talk to us by pinning their ears back, swishing their tails, pawing or stomping their feet, or grinding their teeth. These are efforts on the horse's part to signal us that, 'it hurts' or 'don't do that'.
. Individual long lines of soreness, usually in the middle of the back or near the withers, is most often caused by a crease in the saddle blanket.

If you are experiencing any of these symptoms on a regular basis. Start back checking your saddle-fit or girth/cinch fitting for possible soreness.

Don't overlook good saddle fit - be extra confident that your saddle is fitting. Check with extra care and diligence.

21

SADDLES THAT HAVE A CENTER SEAT SO THE RIDER CAN RIDE OVER THEIR LEGS

ENGLISH SADDLES

GOOD EXAMPLES

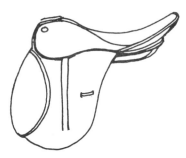

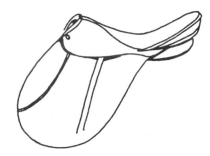

The combination seat, half for jumping and half for general riding.

The dressage and forward seat. Seat pocket and stirrup line are closer together.

WESTERN SADDLES

GOOD EXAMPLES

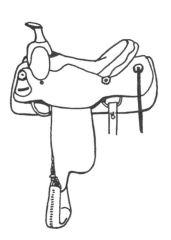

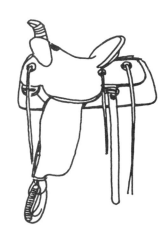

Roper saddle with seat-pocket in middle of saddle. Stirrup line is just ahead of seat pocket. Flat seat.

Old style saddle with some slope to the seat. This style has a smaller seat. Cantle is forward.

EQUITATION OR CHAIR SEAT SADDLES

NOT A GOOD CHOICE

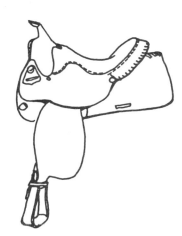

Out of balance or equitation deep seat saddles are not good choices. The seat is not in the middle of the saddle.

The seat is too far back overloading back of the saddle. The stirrup line is too forward to place the legs under the rider.

22

WHEN LOOKING AT USED SADDLES

WEAR SPOTS

**LATIGOS AND
DEE RING TUGS
FRONT AND BACK
BILLETS**

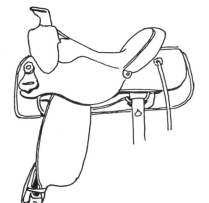

UNDER THE CANTLE ON THE SKIRTS

EDGE OF SEAT JOCKEY--UNDER LEG

RUB AREA BETWEEN SKIRT AND
STIRRUP FENDER AND STIRRUP
LEATHERS

STIRRUP LEATHERS WHERE THE
STIRRUP BAR RUBS

HOW TO BUY

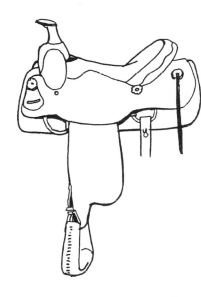

Shop around until you have a 'feel' for new and used saddles in the type you are looking for. Shop the tack stores, the ads in the newspapers, and best of all the tack swaps and auctions. Do not get serious until you have seen all the possibilities on the market.

Next, with a price in mind, talk with the seller and negotiate a price. With used saddles you will have a better chance at adjusting the price to the market.

Things to keep in mind when buying:

1) Saddles made of good quality leathers will last 30 to 50 years so there maybe a good deal of use left in used saddles.
2) Used saddles may need repairs, so you will have to consult with a saddlemaker for repair prices and availability.
3) Ask to try the saddle for a few days...to see if it fits the horse and it fits your riding style. Offer a good deposit and a guarantee against any damage. If not, haul your horse to the saddle and try it for fit. This is the most important part of saddle buying. Don't be 'brow beaten' because if the seller really knows horses he will know how important a proper fit is to the horse's comfort and performance. Don't fall victim to "well is it a full backed Quarter Horse?, or is it part Quarter Horse?, then it will need a semi-quarter horse tree", as if that is all the analysis that is ever needed. Every horse has a different back and the only way to be sure is to try the saddle out.

Try it out without blankets and look and feel under the skirts. But the very best way is to ride the horse with the white pad method, described later, and then for a good trail ride to see if the horse is comfortable and does not develop any sore spots. Especially on the shoulders and under the cantle area.

BUYING CUSTOM SADDLES

Make fitting the saddle to the horse's back and hand carving the 'seat' to fit you (the rider) part of the terms for purchase. Make sure you get it done correctly because this saddle could last you a lifetime of riding, say 50 years. Specify oak bark tanned or vegetable tanned leathers.

Make sure the cinchas or girths are positioned properly for your horse. This is also vital to the position of the saddle on the horse's back for both the horse and rider's comfort.

Adjustable cinch locations are well worth the expense, so you can use the saddle on different horses.

Plate rigging or tug rigging is more secure for heavy work than inskirt 'dees', but it is 'bulkier'. I had a roped yearling bull pull the tree right off the top of the skirts with inskirt rigging. So I prefer the plate, tug, or strap rigging best.

YOUR SADDLEMAKER
CARVES THE GROUND
SEAT FOR YOUR FIT

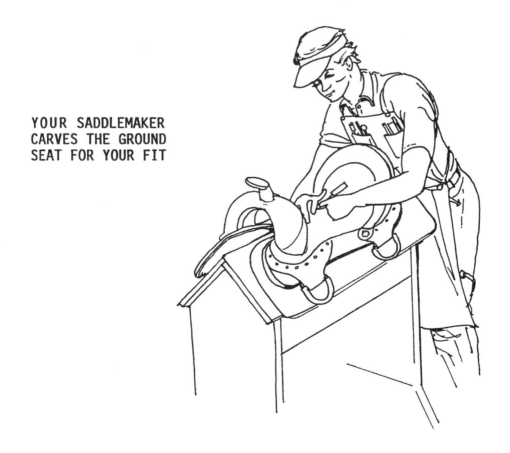

SADDLEMAKERS

The first place to check a poor fit is the 'rocker'.

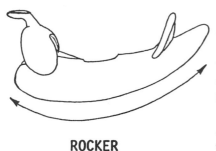

ROCKER

Generally, a mule will not tolerate a poor fitting saddle but a horse will.

Today, saddlemakers do not generally fit the tree to the horse. Saddlemakers, coverers, or upholsterers are not faced with supplying the fit on the horse's back. Their main expertise is applying the leather to a factory made tree. They are not faced with a trade responsibility of fitting the saddle to the horse's back. That is not part of the industry, or their service, or product. Consequently, almost no cencern is given this fact, shifting all the fitting skill to the ability of the factory tree. These trees are built for the 'average' back or biggest share of the market. Today, the majority are built for a semi-quarter or full Quarter Horse back. Unfortunately, most factory trees 'bridge' between the withers and the small of the back and need more 'rocker' or 'swale' to fit behind the withers.

In the 40's and 50's most saddlemakers made the tree as well and fitted the tree to the horse before covering it with leather. Today, 2 x 6's are used instead of 3 x 6's to get the proper 'rocker' in the bars because they are cheaper. Thus, all the bars are the same. Only the cantle and the forks are changed. As a result the horses' backs of today are suffering. Horses are so stoic, they accept the pain and quietly endure their fate. As stewards of their welfare we need to take control and make sure the 'saddle fits'.

A lot of remodeling is possible on the bars, after the skirts have been removed, by adding layers of leather or filing with the rasp. Examine this possibility with your saddlemaker.

Adding leather strips to the bars and then rasping to fit the horse's back. An additional 'stuffed' pad can be sewn on the bottom of the panels of an English saddle to accomplish the same results.

SADDLE LENGTH AND FIT

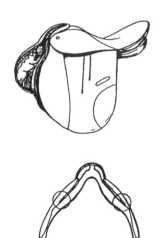

English saddles are likely to be too short and narrow for the weight they have to carry. Plus, the points of the gullet bar must fit correctly. Many pinch or 'flare' and this is critical to proper fit.

The English saddle is one of the worst offenders for fit. In many cases the panels are too narrow for the weight they have to distribute over the tree. Also, most do not have the seat in the middle of the saddle and the bars or tree curve up too much in the back, concentrating the rider's weight in a small area under the cantle.

SADDLE FIT FOR LENGTH

This was shown to me by the U.S. Forest Service packers in Montana in 1948. There are 10 ribs from the back forward, that carry the saddle, a distance of of approximately 18" to 25" in length. Measure the distance with your tape measure from 2" behind the Scapula Hook to the Curve in the Last Rib. Compare it to the length of the saddle bars or tree. Come down off the backbone approximately 8" to make this measurement. Saddles that are too long - Western or English - have nothing substantial to support them beyond this point. The vertebrae that extend out sideways from the backbone beyond this point are several inches below the level of the ribs. In addition, a flexible joint called the CC Joint exists at this point and allows the back and hips to flex up and down and sideways from this point. This motion is consistently hampered by the saddle that is too long, resulting in a sore back at this point.

Measure this distance

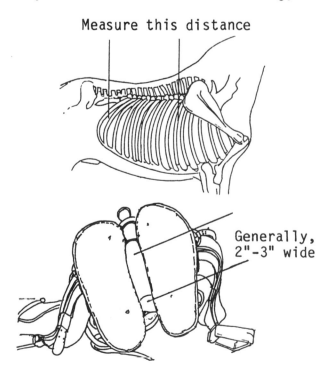

Generally, 2"-3" wide

Locate the back of the Scapula and the 'Hook'. Start from a point 2" behind this point and measure back to the curve in the last rib. This is a fairly hard knot that one can feel with the fingers. Finding the curve of the last rib also takes some searching with the fingers. It is not where the rib goes into the backbone, but where it curves the widest towards the back of the horse. The spread of the saddle bars rests on this area. If the bars are too wide they will cause soreness.

The TUNNEL down the middle of the saddle (on the underside) must <u>not touch the spine</u> (backbone). Further, it must be open enough that it does not compress the blankets and pads onto the backbone. Examine this carefully over the withers.

THE BARS OF THE SADDLE MUST FIT ON TOP OF THE RIB CAGE

The bars of the saddle must fit on the top of the rib cage. The rib cage is slightly flat on the top and then rounds off as it goes down the sides of the horse. The ribs on top have a slight curve to them, as shown below (1). The saddle bars need to be nearly flat, but most are concave. Those curving away from the back (concave) will only sit on part of the back.

If the saddle bars are set too wide, as shown below (2), or are flat and overhang the edge, this can cause soreness along this edge.

Double check this and make sure the saddle is not too wide for the horse in this area.

With the saddle in place examine this fit with your fingers under the saddle or use a tape measure to check the fit.

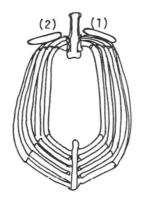 

Front view of rib cage   Top view with saddle bars

FOOTPRINT OF THE SADDLE BARS

Most trees do not fit because the Rocker, the Rafter or the Twist is incorrect.

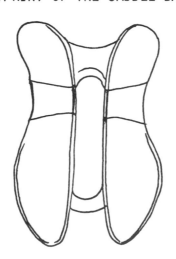

Fits in the pocket beside the withers

Narrows in the shoulders

Widens in the loin area

If the gullet does not fit, you have a no fit - do not go any further.

Back of bars do not ride over the last rib and curve up

Sits down evenly on the back the entire length

HOW THE BARS FIT THE HORSE

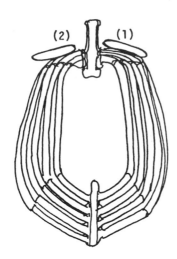

FRONT VIEW OF RIB CAGE
On (1) the bar fits for rafter and gullet width, so the bar sits on top of the rib cage. On (2), bar is overhanging and will make the back sore on the outside of the rib cage. The rafter appears okay, but the gullet width is too wide. A narrower gullet needs to be selected out of the 5 Standard Back styles generally offered in trees.

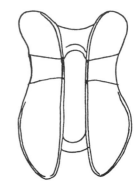

FOOTPRINT OF BARS
The bars are made to ride on top of the rib cage.

TOP VIEW OF THE BARS ON THE RIB CAGE
Note the spread sets wider in the back. The bars are also specially shaped to fit into the withers up front, but the length is also very important.

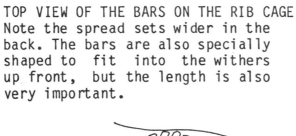

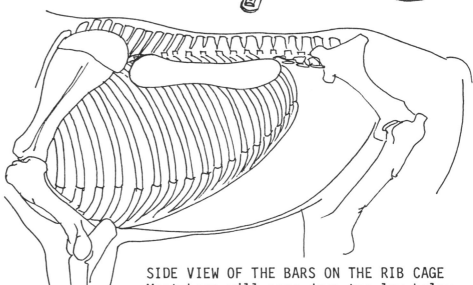

Make sure the gullet channel is wide enough so as not to 'squeeze' the backbone. A couple of inches wide on each side of the spine is normal.

SIDE VIEW OF THE BARS ON THE RIB CAGE
Most bars will come down too low below the scapula hook (farthest point back on scapula). The withers pocket does not extend much below the scapula hook. Low bars overhang the rib cage, as mentioned above, so proper gullet width selection is important. Make sure the bars do not fit over or below the withers pocket.

LOCATING THE SADDLE
OVER THE LOW SPOT ON THE HORSE'S BACK

Locating the low spot, or the seat, of the saddle on the low spot of the back of the horse is vital, so the rider can ride balanced over the Center of Gravity of the horse.

Most saddles are 6" to 10" behind this point. This has two other features: (1) it is the center of motion of the horse like the center of a teeter-totter where it is the smoothest place to ride, and (2) it is the best place for the horse to carry your weight.

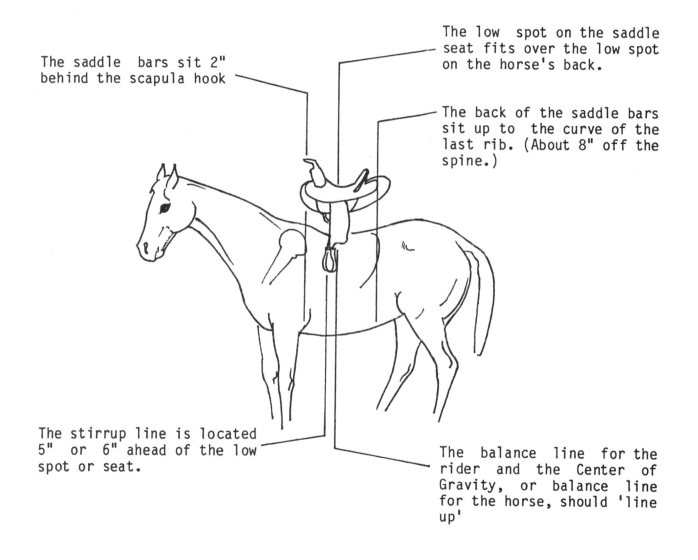

The saddle bars sit 2" behind the scapula hook

The low spot on the saddle seat fits over the low spot on the horse's back.

The back of the saddle bars sit up to the curve of the last rib. (About 8" off the spine.)

The stirrup line is located 5" or 6" ahead of the low spot or seat.

The balance line for the rider and the Center of Gravity, or balance line for the horse, should 'line up'

The placement of the seat, or 'low spot', is the responsibility of the saddlemaker. When the strainer seat is put in, the low spot is controlled by the saddlemaker. It is not entirely the design of the tree that controls this location.

THE WITHERS CONTROL THE LENGTH OF THE SADDLE

Flat withered horses will take longer saddles.

High withered horses will take shorter saddles.

2" BACK OF THE
SCAPULA HOOK TO
THE CURVE IN
THE LAST RIB.

The distance from 2" in back of the scapula hook to the curve in the last rib is longer on low withered horses. The shoulders are generally straighter and the withers set farther forward on the back.

Horses with larger withers and are deeper in the back have more of a sloping-back-angle to the shoulder and correspondingly the withers set farther into the back. This makes the back shorter. These type of backs take more of a "rocker" curve to the bottom of the bars to fit into the distinct swale.

IMPORTANT: THE BARS
MUST BE THE CORRECT
LENGTH. MOST BARS
ARE TOO LONG.

Different breeds are going to require different length saddles. Most Quarter Horse trees, like roping saddles, are too long for many other breeds.

So, your first step, in locating a saddle that fits, is to measure from 2" behind the scapula hook to the curve in the last rib. This controls the length of the bars in looking for a saddle that fits.

Now measure the length of the saddle bars on your prospective saddle selection. They should be very close to matching.

Too long will cause soreness in the deep back of the horse, especially horses that are worked athletically.

FIVE TYPES OF HORSE'S BACKS

THE FULL QUARTER HORSE BACK. Gullet size: 6-1/2" to 7" Low rocker. Extra and flat rafter. Wide gullet channel. Wider bars and long back. The bars are 14" wide under the gullet. Use full double cinch.

LOCATING THE CINCH
The withers, scapula and the elbow dictate the location of the cinch.

Saddle 2" behind the scapula.

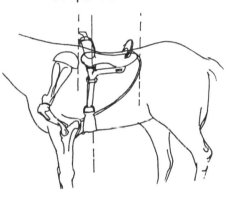

Cinch rings are 3" back and 3" up from the elbow, then up to the saddle. This locates the saddle.

Egg crate pads help take the heavy jerk on the shoulders. Get your saddle maker to help you seat the bars into the skirts.

One needs to become familiar with the horse's back before launching into a saddle selection. A quick glance at the back in question is easily answered using the following five types. The reason there are five types is these are the traditional types that tree manufacturers build.

The first type is a FULL QUARTER HORSE and it takes a FULL QUARTER HORSE TREE. This type has a full flat set of withers with very wide shoulders, heavy muscling along the backbone and somewhat flat over the last rib. In many cases the croup is higher than the withers. Thus, this type of back requires special rocker to allow for the flat rise in the back. Double cinching with the back cinch taken up is required to keep the saddle flat and stop any brushing (rubbing the loin).

If the back has considerable 'swale' behind the withers, then it will need extra rocker in the bars. Measure and shape the back with your plumbers tape or plaster gauze, as described in this book. If the back tips up to the croup, then sometimes a 'britchen' under the tail helps hold the saddle from working up on the scapula. 'Shimming' the withers with pads is not advised. A full sized tapered pad may help if one can be located, something to keep the saddle from crawling up on the withers and soring up these critical muscles.

The back legs look longer than the fronts and the horse is 'front loaded' with well sprung ribs.

This back usually has a straight shoulder which means the withers are farther forward and thus, requires a full double, 7/8, or 3/4 rigging. The reason for the full double rigging "D's" is to hold the saddle down flat over the entire back and hold it in a proper position behind the withers. Backs of this type are hard to hold the saddle in place and are usually over cinched, especially when going up or down hill, getting off and on, or roping. Ropers with this type of back are better off using a blanket and one good thick pad to cushion the concussion from the 'jerk'. Extra heavy skirting leather is advisable for roping saddles. One can take heavy leather shims the size of the skirts and add them to the skirts, glue and sew them on then replace the fleece or sheepskin. This helps.

QUARTER HORSE BACK. Gullet size: 6-1/4" to 6-1/2". Bar width bottom 13-1/2". Use full double, 7/8 or 3/4 rigging.

The second type back is not as flat withered as the Full Quarter Horse Back and generally the backbone is more predominately revealed. The shoulders are usually wide and the width of the withers is wide. It may have a fairly straight shoulder, but not always. The ribs are generally well sprung and quite flat over the loin. Some maybe a little higher in the croup, but this also varies. It does reveal an extra width across the back and it will be longer from the scapula to the last rib, possibly 20" to 24".

This is a very common back. The withers and the contour over the last rib will describe this style back.

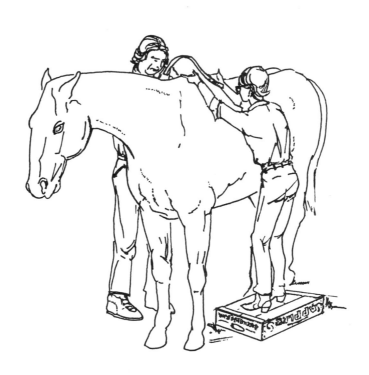

Shaping the plumber's tape is a two man job

SEMI-QUARTER HORSE BACK. This is the most common back. The gullet size is 5-1/2" to 6-1/2". The rafter varies from flat to semi-sloped over the back ribs. It has a distinct rocker and can be rigged at 7/8, 3/4, or 5/8 for proper placement of the cinch. Bottom of front bars near 13" wide.

The third type is a big category of backs and may have a good set of withers, wide or narrow shoulders, a flat or swayed back, and flat or sloping ribs at the croup. Generally the withers are higher than the croup and the spine is fairly level. It is classified as a SEMI-QUARTER HORSE BACK in the United States. This calls for extra 'twist' and 'flat' raftering for the back of the saddle.

In addition, pay close attention to the width of the withers, your plumbers tape or plaster gauze will help you here. Also, pay attention to the 'travel-back' of of the scapula so it will not hit the forward portion of the saddle tree. The scapula rear-motion is more predominate with higher, deep withered horses because the scapula tips back farther.

Place the saddle two fingers behind the scapula hook and generally this requires a 7/8, 3/4, or 5/8 rigging or cinch rigging to accommodate the 'deeper withers' and deep elbow.

The variations to look for come in the width of the shoulders, the flatness of the back, and the length of the rib cage. Your 3 measurements will tell you this.

STANDARD BACK. Gullet width is 5-1/4" to 5-3/4". Generally distinct rocker and average rafter at 13" across bottom of bars. Rigged: 3/4 to 5/8 . The bars need a little more spread in back to rest on the ribs.

The fourth big type of backs are STANDARD BACKS and they are characterized with common withers and with average slope and width to the rib cage. This may not be average to some folks, but until the advent of the Quarter Horse, in the late 40's and 50's, this was the average back (thinner horse).

These type backs maybe longer and narrower with some horses than others. One distinction with this type of back is the shoulders are most often narrower than the Quarter Horse backs. Thus, calling for a narrower gullet selection. Approximately 6-1/4" to 6-1/2" wide inside the gullet from the conchas.

Sometimes this style of back may slope downhill to the croup and a breast collar is advisable to hold the saddle forward. The vary shape of the withers pushes the saddle back.

Another distinction is the backs are not as well sprung or as wide as most Quarter Horses and the ribs tend to have slightly more slope. This calls for a little narrower rafter.

WIDE BACKED ARABS. Usually 6-1/4" to 6-1/2" in the gullet. Bottom of front bars 13" to 13-1/2" wide. Bars length 18" to 19". 3/4 to 5/8 rigged.

The fifth type of backs is WIDE BACKED ARABS. Many Arabs have a back like the Semi-Quarter Horse Back, but with a shorter rib cage. It maybe only 18" to 19" long. This requires a shorter set of bars, yet a wide gullet and good rafter with a good amount of twist. Most have a flat back with well sprung ribs and an occasional higher croup.

3/4 to 5/8 rigging is often the best choice. The Arab has a lot of travel 'back' of the scapula and this should be noted that it does not 'hit' into the front bars of the saddle.

Both Western and English manufacturers have the 5 basic styles.

Most English saddles have too much rafter (too narrow) in the gullet to fit the withers and shoulders. These typically sit very high. With this type the points of the gullet bar dig into the sides of the shoulders and create real discomfort.

Trees are not categorized by breed. This is unfortunate because most breeds have some common characteristics.

The Western Stock saddles built for ranchers during the late 40's and 50's on Semi-Quarter Horse trees have shorter bars and work very well on Arab backs. The saddles were very popular with northern ranchers and still are today.

WARM BLOOD BACKS

Many of these horses call for a Quarter Horse tree or a Semi-Quarter Horse tree, but with very little rocker. These trees, by definition, are also available in English trees.

JUDGING THE BACK

Getting up higher than the rump and looking forward to the withers gives you a good view of the back.

SHOPPING FOR A SADDLE THAT FITS

Fitting horse's backs is more uniform than might be guessed, but there are those that are not considered common that represent a large number. The Quarter Horse Style Tree is built to fit the majority of backs and anything different or with withers presents a bit of a problem for the 'tree' industry.

Flat faced bars are the preference of many professionals (that is across the surface of the bars, than those convex).

Also, center seats or pockets in the middle of the saddle are the preference of many professionals. Those with the sitrrups too far forward overload the front of the saddle.

THE FIRST STEP
MEASUREMENTS TO
TAKE SHOPPING

The conformation of the front of the saddle determines the fit of the saddle, so in fitting the saddle, extra care must be taken to achieve a proper fit over the withers and onto the shoulders.

FIT AND BAR SPREAD

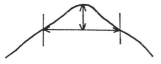

Take the shape 2" behind the scapula hook.

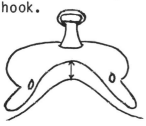

Critical area to observe - contact area under bars

Use some heavy wire or plumbers tape to sculpt a pattern of the surface 2" behind the scapula hook. Remove the wire, then measure down from the top approximately 3-1/2" (as shown in the illustration), then measure across from this point. It will read something like 5-1/2" to 7-1/2" wide. This will give you an 'idea' of the gullet width that you are looking for.

Take your shaped wire with you as you shop for saddles and fit it into the throat or gullet for comparison. Remember, the top of the wire should be set something like 3" to 3-1/2" below the inside of the gullet (as shown). This allows for clearance for the withers and room for blankets.

The final test is to try the saddle on the horse with blankets for the best test. Do not buy until you try.

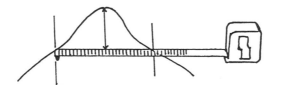

Measure down 3" to 3-1/2". Next, measure across.

Your shaped wire or tape will be approximately 24" to 30" long. Fit the wire flush to the withers-pocket 2" behind the scapula hook.

Also, measure and sculpt a piece of tape for the back of the saddle. Take both along when you go saddle shopping.

FITTING THE SADDLE TO THE HORSE'S BACK

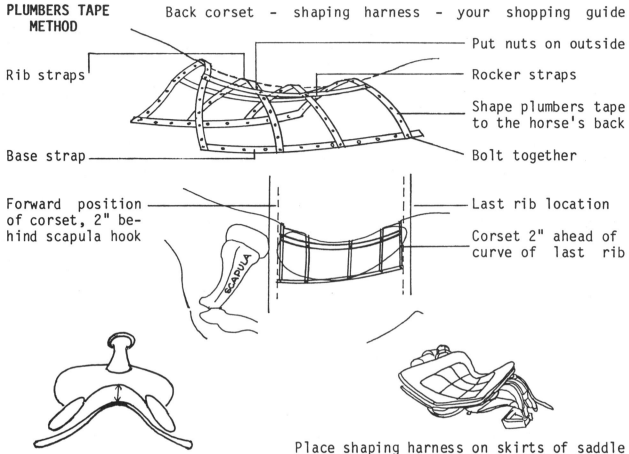

PLUMBERS TAPE METHOD

Back corset - shaping harness - your shopping guide

Rib straps

Put nuts on outside

Rocker straps

Shape plumbers tape to the horse's back

Base strap

Bolt together

Forward position of corset, 2" behind scapula hook

Last rib location

Corset 2" ahead of curve of last rib

Allow 2" to 3" above the harness to the underside of the swells.

Place shaping harness on skirts of saddle to measure fit. Align with front of bars. Add a pad for a better look at the fit.

Materials needed are: 1" plumbers tape (available at your building center), 15 1/2" x 1/4" bolts, nuts and washers (available at your hardware store). Shape 4 or 5 ribs as shown and bolt onto the base-strap at the bottom and onto the top ridge-straps. The first rib-strap is 2" behind the 'scapula-hook' and the last strap is 2" ahead of the curve in the last rib of the horse's back. 10" down each side is usually long enough to measure the shape of the saddle bars.

Be careful not to bend the harness once you have it shaped and bolted together. Next place it onto the bottom side of the saddle skirts to measure the fit. Place the first strap-rib on the front edge of the saddle bars in the throat of the saddle. The 'shapes' must marry up or it is not a fit. No fudging or compromises because it is a good looking saddle!

When you place the harness on the skirts you should show nearly 2" to 3" to the underside of the gullet or throat of the swells. When adding the blanket and pad it will push the throat or gullet up some because of their thickness. On the horse it should measure a good 3" over the withers.

PLASTER GAUZE METHOD

It is easy
to handle.

Makes a good
shopping guide.

This is another way of measuring the horse's back that maybe a little easier for some. This is to use PLASTER GAUZE made for casting broken bones on humans. This is laid out and structured just like the plumbers tape harness only using the plaster gauze. Some gauzes only have to be dipped in water to harden, others harden when exposed to the air. It is available at medical supply houses, etc. (see your telephone yellow pages for your area).

The gauze is available in rolls approximately 3" wide by 3' long at a cost of about $2.75 each. Place strips of the gauze on the horse's back in a similar fashion as shown with the plumbers tape corset. Let the strips harden, usually this takes 15 minutes or so, then remove for a 'shopping pattern'. This will give you a 'preliminary' study of the shape of the horse's back. The white pad test makes the final evaluation.

HANDLE WITH CARE
IN TRANSPORTING

It has several drawbacks not found with the plumbers tape in that it may break or bend easier. Be careful in trasnporting it. Also, the horse will move around in the 15 minutes it takes to dry and cause some minor distortion.

If it is cold outside, it may take longer to fit and harden and this could cause problems.

If available, check the saddle with a pad.

Use the gauze harness
with a pad to check
the fit.

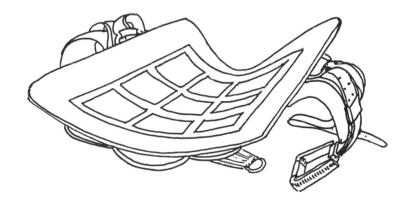

THE FLOUR METHOD

Leave the
blankets
off

Dust the skirts
or take them off
and dust the bars

Another method is to dust the bottom of the saddle skirts or tree bars (testing the bars is best) with flour or chalk. Then using a damp towel go over the horse's back lightly so the flour will stick to it. Then place the saddle straight down on the horse's back, press lightly, then <u>lift</u> straight up and off.

The flour from the bottom of the saddle skirts or tree bars will leave a white print, where they touched the back, and leave it bare where they didn't. This will give you a pretty good indication if the saddle is fitting well or not. If the fleece on the bottom of the saddle is new and sticking way 'up' it does not work as well.

Be liberal with the flour and if you are testing the tree bars you may have to wet the bottom surface of the tree first before putting on the flour...or it won't stick.

Get a tall person to put the saddle on or use a good step ladder so you can lift the saddle straight up so it won't smudge.

Look especially for a gap in coverage between the back of the withers and the small of the back.

**DUST THE BOTTOM OF
THE SADDLE SKIRTS
OR THE TREE BARS**

38

PUTTING THE SADDLE
STRAIGHT DOWN - THEN
LIFT IT STRAIGHT UP

DON'T MOVE IT AROUND
OR IT WILL SMUDGE

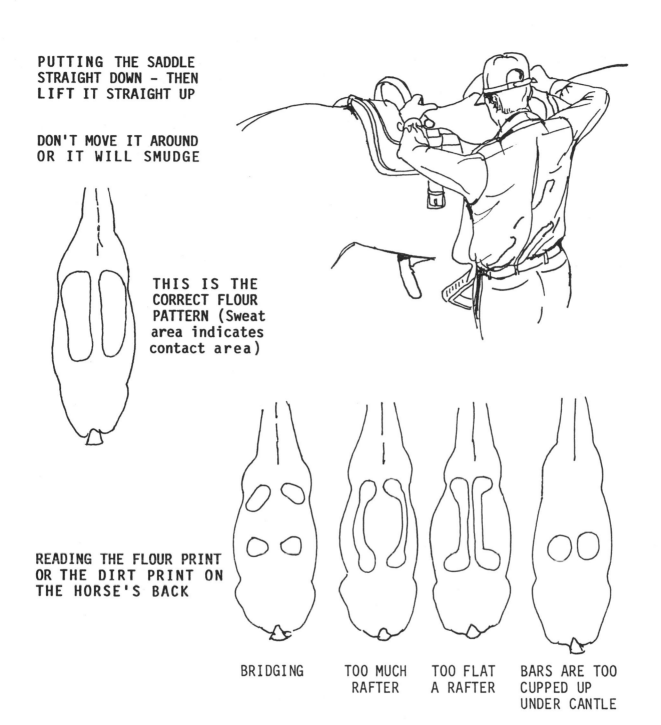

THIS IS THE
CORRECT FLOUR
PATTERN (Sweat
area indicates
contact area)

READING THE FLOUR PRINT
OR THE DIRT PRINT ON
THE HORSE'S BACK

BRIDGING   TOO MUCH   TOO FLAT   BARS ARE TOO
            RAFTER   A RAFTER   CUPPED UP
                                      UNDER CANTLE

You can reshape the bars either by rasping or by building up the surface with layers of leather and then shaping them with a rasp. Details shown on later pages.

NOTE WHEN
UNSADDLING

A dry spot on the horse's back, such as the shoulders or loin area, means excessive pressure or none at all. It can mean that there is so much pressure it won't sweat or the bars are not hitting at all. The contact areas are shown by the flour print under normal pressure. More on dry spots later.

THE WHITE PAD METHOD

THE WHITE PAD METHOD SHOWS THE AREAS OF PRESSURE

A very effective method, once you have the saddle in hand, is to use the WHITE PAD METHOD TO TEST THE FIT. The White Pad is a 1/2-inch white orthopedic pad, or something comparable, and a regular saddle blanket that folds into 1/2-inch thick and is placed over the top of the white pad. This is equal to the thickness of most pads and blankets when you ride. This is important.

RUB THE CHALK IN EVENLY ALL OVER THE BACK. Use Carpenter's Line Chalk (Red or Blue).

The first step is to rub a generous amount of colored carpenters chalk onto the horse's back in the area where the saddle rides. Next, place the white pad on the back and then the blanket over the pad. Now saddle the horse with the saddle to be tested.

Next, ride the horse for 15 or 20 minutes making sure to walk, trot, and lope the horse along with some sharp rollbacks and circles.

Next, remove the pad and examine the underside of the pad.

NEXT, ADD THE WHITE PAD WITH THE BLANKET ON TOP.

A Print Out made by the chalk will be on the bottom of the pad. Where there are dark stains, the pad is receiving maximum pressure from the footprint of the saddle tree or bars. Where it is a middle tone, it is just getting normal contact. Some areas may show 'brushing' near the outside edges from the horse's movement. Where there is no color (or white), it is not getting any contact. Solid dark and opaque areas indicate excessive pressure and may blister. White areas behind the withers would indicate 'bridging' and the saddle is not fitting.

Sitting on the back of the saddle will distort the print-out. It puts too much pressure on the back.

A pressure scale is, as follows:

1+	100% coverage - opaque areas:	<u>Excess pressure</u>
1	75% coverage, but not as solid:	<u>Unacceptable</u>
2	50% coverage, medium color:	<u>Heavy</u>
3	Less than 50% color:	<u>Moderate</u>
4	Less than 25% color (pad looks ruffed up):	<u>Light brushing</u>

EXAMPLES OF THIS METHOD ARE SHOWN ON THE FOLLOWING PAGES

Most of the footprint should be 2's and 3's with 4's along the outside edges and over the back on the loin where there is movement. See the following pages.

BEFORE WE LOOK AT THE WHITE PAD,
LET'S LOOK AT THE HORSE'S BACK:

This is a Blue Chalk Study made on the back of a
grey Arab gelding, 15 hands, 1,000 pounds, with good
withers, short back, well sprung ribs, and medium to
heavy shoulders. Following a good ride we removed the
saddle and pad. An illustration of the back is shown
below:

ILLUSTRATION OF
THE HORSE'S BACK
Western Saddle

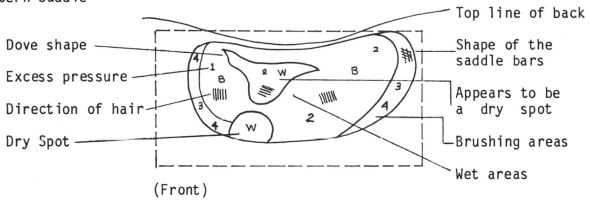

Dove shape

Excess pressure

Direction of hair

Dry Spot

Top line of back

Shape of the
saddle bars

Appears to be
a dry spot

Brushing areas

Wet areas

(Front)

DOVE SHAPE

The dove shaped area does not
appear to sweat as much as the
surrounding area.

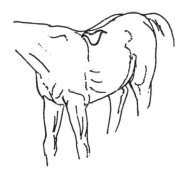

The 'Dove' shape on the back is partly due to the fact
that a Ligamentous Facia covers this muscle area and
does not sweat or move as readily as the area surrounding it. The hair direction shows that there is
not much movement, whereas near the outside of the
bars there is considerable movement.

This area maybe mistaken for a no pressure area, or no
contact area, or one that has excessive pressure. An
observer must be very careful here. The only way to
actually be sure is to use the white pad and blue
chalk method. One cannot tell from observation whether
it is a pressure area or a no pressure area. If it is
starting to swell or blister, then it obviously is a
pressure area, or if it is very sore to the touch, but
otherwise, I can't tell. So I go to the next step and
use the blue chalk and white pad method to be sure.

Compare this pattern made on the horse's back to the
white pad examples on the following pages.

41

EXAMPLE OF THE WHITE PAD TEST WITH 1/2" PAD AND 1/2" BLANKET

This is a pad print out on the same grey Arab gelding using the blue chalk, 1/2" orthopedic pad, and a 1/2" Navajo blanket on top. The ride lasted over 20 minutes.

Drawing showing the blue chalk printed onto the white pad.

#1+   Excessive

#1   Unacceptable

#2   Heavy

#3   Moderate

#4   Light Brushing

Looking at the underside of the white pad.

(Front)

COMMENTS:

A) #1+ areas show excess on bars behind withers. The #1 areas must go!

B) #1 areas show on small of back. Shows some bridging (front to back).

C) Bars are making adequate contact as #2 areas show.

CORRECTIONS:

A) Saddler could add leather to the bottom of the bars. Needs more rocker, 1/4" or so.

B) Saddle bars could be too long (?) Need to check.

C) Could skive-off and round-up front of bars, but this would ruin the tree.

The saddle is still bridging, but can be corrected.

The right bar on the withers still shows an excess area of coverage because the back is uneven. The horse is possibly left leaded (over developed) thus tipping the saddle to the offside bar.

This saddle is worth correcting with the #2 pressure indicated all along the bars - this is acceptable. Leather add-ons to the tree bars just behind the withers and 'feathered' out over an 8" to 10" area will make this saddle workable.

ARAB BACKS

Saddle fitting Arabs always seems to retain some 'brushing' character to the small of the back, this will be true in this case. Also, the #1 pressure under the cinch/girth billets will probably go away with the add-ons to the bottom of the tree.

THIS IS THE UNDER-
SIDE OF THE WHITE
PAD MARKED WITH
BLUE CHALK FROM
THE HORSE ON THE
PREVIOUS PAGE.

#1+   Excessive

#1   Unacceptable

#2   Heavy

#3   Moderate

#4   Light Brushing

NOTES:

COMMENTS: STUDY OF
THE PRINT OUT ABOVE

The dove area
shows pressure

DO NOT USE THICK
PADS WITH THE
WHITE PAD FOR
THIS TEST

THE WHITE PAD TEST WITH TOO MANY PADS

Shown below is a read out of the same back with the
chalk method using a fleece pad and a white pad. (Put
chalk on evenly over the entire surface.)

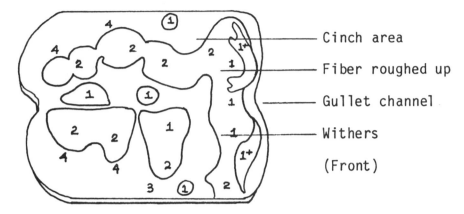

— Cinch area

— Fiber roughed up

— Gullet channel

— Withers

(Front)

Fabric over withers roughed up.
Fabric over loin area smooth, same as hair direction.
Pressure on spine and withers probably caused by fleece
pad (1-1/2" thick).

You will notice, first off, that there is solid blue,
or #2 areas, that show coverage in the 'Dove' area.
The blue pad shows the saddle fits adequately in this
area. One must be very careful that the saddle is not
bridging, in this case, between the withers and the
loin area. If a thick fleece pad is used over the white
pad, as in this case, it will fill in the depressions
making it show #2 blue on the white pad. So, it is important not to use thick fleece pads for this test. We
did use it to illustrate the effect.

Notice the markings under the cinch rings ('D's) on the
horse's back are now also #2 blue areas, but showed
white or dry on the horse's back (Illustration #1).

Also, notice that there is a graduation of blue inten-
sity starting with the #2 on the spine, gradually
turning into #3's moving away from the spine, then
along the outside edges of the bars #4's or brushing.
(This is due in part to the fact the bars are sculpted
up or rounded on the edges.) It could also be that the
rafter is too low.

Another aspect of this print out on the white pad is
there are #1 areas in two places on the spine. This
cannot be an acceptable fit. The fleece pad is too
thick over the spine. In this case, use a pad that
is 'jointed' in the middle (thinner).

43

Those areas shaped like bananas on the leading edges of the saddle bars showing #1+ (excessive pressure) are not acceptable either. This possibly could be caused by the extra thick fleece pad. The front of the bars can be filed up rounder and possibly eliminate this pressure.

If #1's were shown under the swells or forks and it sat 3" or so over the spine, it would mean the pads were too thick or the gullet was too small (narrow).

NO CONTACT AREA   The white channel on the (nearside forward) above the cinch 'D' rings indicates no contact. This is due partly to the fact that the horse appears more developed on the nearside and it is 'dumping' the saddle off to the right or offside.

The correction for this would be to work the horse more to the right and enlarge these muscles or add leather strips to the tree bars in this area.

The area right under the 'cinch rings or 'D's' will always show #2's, but #1's are not acceptable.

READING THE WHITE PAD   Reading the white pad can reveal a lot of fitting problems. An acceptable fit is one that shows the most even distribution of weight over the entire bar surface. No contact areas or excessive pressure areas are not acceptable. Large gaps or large differences between one side and the other are also not acceptable.

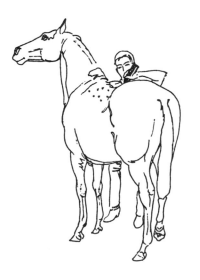

Dusting the back with the carpenters line chalk.

Place the white pad first and then the blanket on the chalked area, then saddle the horse.

OTHER METHODS:

HIGH TECH METHOD OF FITTING

There is a computer saddle fitting company that features a pressure sensitive pad that goes on under the saddle. It records this information on a 'lap top' monitor in the degrees of pressure exerted by the bars. In addition, a rider can be added to study the distribution of the weight over the bars. It shows if the rider is in the middle of the saddle or out of balance.

This unit will help you locate the concentrations of pressure and the rider's weight effect.

It appears the 'cinching or girth' pressure is added to the rider's weight and this causes excess pressure to be indicated on the monitor. The cinch/girth pressure pulls the saddle down into the horse's back on the front end and raises the back end. In addition, it will not tell you if the shape of the tree is correct, only the high and low areas of pressure.

BACKYARD TECHNOLOGY

Another method is to use a light horse blanket or pad and soak it in plaster of paris (found in art stores) and place it on the horse's back. Let it dry, then remove it and use it as your model for selecting a saddle that is close to a fit. Mark the pad so you can tell where the saddle 'sits' in relationship to the back. Then when you study different saddles you will have it in the right location. The advantage here is, it is easier to haul the pad than the horse to the saddle shop.

OLD TIMERS METHOD

A very sound and fundamental way to test fit is to re-move the saddle skirts from the proposed saddle, then fit the saddle on the horse's back and study it by eye. This works! (With English saddles this is not necessary.) If the skirts are nailed on rather than held on with the strings, as in custom saddles, this is hard to do. You can 'chalk' the tree and place it on the back for an accurate readout.

HOW TO NOTICE POOR FIT. WATCH THEM WHEN THEY ROLL AFTER A RIDE

After you ride, go let the horse roll in soft dirt and where the dirt sticks on the sweaty parts you can see the areas that are dry. This is where the saddle is not fitting. One can powder the back with dry dirt and see the same thing. The hair, where it is wet, sort of 'sticks-up'. This is a good preliminary way to detect poor fit. Then use the methods above to study the fit further.

Of the various methods described for saddle fit I like the use of the plumbers tape first - as a preliminary test - then, second use the blue or red chalk method onto a white pad, followed by a good long ride. This takes 3 steps, but it seems to work for me.

I have tried the other methods, but have my best success working this way.

There is no way that I know of for fitting saddles that is full proof. It cannot be done...because the back is always changing with the flexing of the muscles when in motion. The long muscle, or Latissimus Dorse, flexes to open the stride, then the shorter stomach muscles, that support the ribs and abdomen, contract and pull the legs back under the horse. Thus, you have two major muscle groups working - first one, then the other, continually. The back has something like 12 layers of muscles all working controlling a purposeful function. But the bars should - fit the basic shape of the back. The rocker, the rafter, the twist, and the rounded edges should be shaped correctly for the standing back.

The computer method seems to give an extra measure accounting for the effect of the cinching or girth pressure. While other methods of shaping the back with calipers or templates does not work out as accurately as the plumbers tape for me.

PADS

The various pads that are now coming onto the market will not make a saddle fit - but can be helpful in 'fine-tuning' the fit. You cannot pad out a bad fit. If you have too little or too much rocker, or too little or too much rafter, or the twist is not correct, or the saddle bars are too long - you must correct these or you do not have a fit.

CINCHING OR GIRTH
PRESSURE   ON   THE
FRONT OF THE SADDLE

3/4, 5/8 rigging on plate rigging has less of this effect

When the saddle is cinched, or girthed up and the billets are well forward, it pulls only the front half of the saddle down into the muscles of the back, maybe a 1/2-inch or so. This causes the saddle to ride up in back. When the rider gets on it leverages even more pressure on the front half with the rider's weight. Forward cinches should have the rear cinches also drawn up to compensate for this effect. Billets in front and back onto one 'D' are advantageous.

| READING THE CINCHING EFFECT | The areas around the cinch billets show a #1 and this is too high. However, with the use of a second cinch this maybe eliminated. |

THE CINCHING EFFECT USING TWO CHINCHES

Outside the U.S. many countries use front and back bil- lets to one 'D', or an over-cinch, to correct his problem

The cinching effect is to pull the saddle down and tip it forward as it pulls the tree down into the relaxed muscles under the front of the saddle. So, as the front is pulled down, perhaps a half-inch into the back, the back of the saddle now tips up, say a half-inch, with no pressure on the horse.

It is often prudent to use two cinches if you are sad- dling horses with low withers, or if you notice this effect. Also, it is prudent not to over cinch a horse, just fairly snug will do. If you have a good fit, this is easier. It makes it easier for the horse to move and breathe.

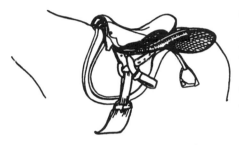

3/4 to 5/8 with flat plate rigging will not produce this effect as dramatically as 7/8 to a full double. It is a good practice to bring up your back cinch to hold the back of the saddle down. This 'evens' out the distribution of pressure over the back.

If the stirrups are too far forward they just add to this overloading effect on the withers. The stirrups placed farther back helps even out the pressure evenly over the entire undersurface of the bars. 5" or 6" ahead of the center of the seat seems to work best.

PUMP HANDLE EFFECT

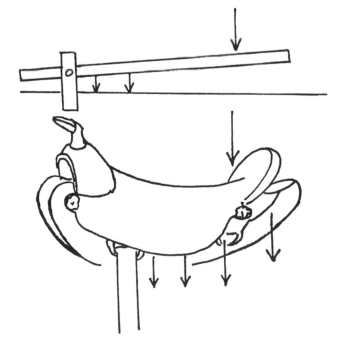

Taking a long ride as the last step in selecting a saddle

The last step in selecting a saddle is to take a good hard ride for two hours, or preferably longer, to justify whether the saddle works with the horse's back when the horse is in motion, doing the things that you normally do when you use the horse. The static position, with the tree or saddle placed on the horse's back, gives you about half the picture. That is why it is so important to actually work the horse with the prospective saddle on board.

I like to saddle the horse with a clean pad, one that I can read off the bottom just as with the White Pad Method, but this time without the chalk. If there are areas rubbing, or taking too much pressure, not only will the back (likely) get sore, but it will show up on the clean pad. Be sure to palpate the back, with 'surface' and 'deep' soreness in mind, after the ride.

Saddles are not perfect

Western and English saddles are not perfect, even when you get a really good fit. But it is the best anyone can do with stiff trees. A good fit generally is acceptable, but sometimes improvements need to be made to account for the 'shaping' that occurs from the horse in motion. Here the White Pad can help you again fine tune the bars or panels to work with the horse in motion.

I often find that the saddle fits standing, but the front of the bars are digging into the withers. So, I have rasped off and rounded up the bars on several saddles and it works.

Again, check the fit of the gullet

Besides bridging, the next most common failure of saddle fit is the gullet is too narrow or too wide for the horse. This causes pinching on the muscles working over the withers, for the forearm and the neck and the back - effecting them all. Measuring, or scoping out, a fit with the plumbers tape shows how important a step this can be. Place your blanket and pad on the saddle when checking this fit.

THE PREFERRED METHOD OF
SELECTING A SADDLE COMES DOWN TO THESE STEPS:

1) Shape your tapes to the horse (plumbers tape shaping corset).

2) Finding the saddle in the market that fits your budget, the corset, and it fits you.

3) Buy the saddle with a return guarantee, or on a trial basis with a deposit (say, $100.00). If it fits the horse you will buy it. If it does not, you will return it - in as good of shape as it was when it left.

4) Try the saddle with the White Pad or Flour Fitting Technique on the horse. It works or it does not work.

5) If it works, try the saddle on the horse for a good long ride, read out the pad, then palpate the back when you are done. If it fits, no soreness. If it does not fit, you will more than likely have soreness.

6) Buy or take the saddle back.

Study the back for soreness

49

DRY SPOTS

There are 2 types.
This is from my
experience.

DRY SPOTS after unsaddling are found in two types: from EXCESSIVE PRESSURE and NO PRESSURE. Pressure Dry Spots are usually on or behind the withers or over the loin. No Pressure Dry Spots are usually behind the withers caused from bridging. Excess pressure areas may not sweat. The No Pressure areas are usually larger areas and tend to run the long way.

Sometimes sweat-blister or sheet blister areas are called DRY SPOTS. Technically, this is not correct. Blister areas have excessive pressure.

Those Dry Spots with excess pressure will have heat and will be slightly sweaty. (A baby's forehead thermometer will indicate this.) In a few minutes, it generally will sweat more, but start to dry and the effect tapers off. If the process continues, it will become a permanent injury, showing white hair near the bottom of the damaged area. After unsaddling, a blister or seroma starts to form, this is an inflammatory reaction. If severe enough, fibrosis tissue will form and damage the pigmentation cells causing white hair to start to grow. This is similar to 'freeze branding'.

PREVENTION
Get a saddle
that fits.
Check the backbone.
Injury here can
cause a fistula and
these are extremely
hard to cure.
Out of shape horses
tend to blister
easier.

Your best prevention is palpate the back (or test with your fingers for soreness) under the saddle contact areas. Any soreness is a sign of a possible blister. Continued use will scar and white hair will develop, not to mention the adverse reaction from the horse and its dramatic drop in performance.

At first, you will not see the blister - as the saddle comes off - but after a while, when the back dries, you will (possibly) see the blister start. The blister may not show for sometime, in the beginning, but the soreness will.

CURE
You can continue
to ride the horse
if you use a riding
pad with stirrups
and cinch.

If you detect a sore area with your fingers or brush, get cold water on the site, such as out of the hose or a cold compress, for a good 15-minutes or more. Anti-inflammatory drugs maybe used, but wear-off in several days and likely fibrosis will continue. The use of pressure on the site MUST STOP - the horse needs rest and a proper fitting saddle. This may take several weeks for healing. Palpate (feel) the back after every ride just as a matter of course - the Cavalry required this and all old ranchers and packers did too. On long rides it's good to wash the back with a sponge, after unsaddling, to remove the salt that can act as an abrasive on future rides.

SADDLE FIT IS EX-TREMELY IMPORTANT

With pads/blankets you need sweat absorption and air.

Saddle fit is 90% the cure and pads and blankets are the rest. Uneven backs are a factor to check. Blankets that wrinkle from crawling, or climb into the gullet channel, or do not cool the back will also cause blistering. Wool blankets and horse hair or felt pads work best.

DRY SPOTS UNDER THE SADDLE

Dry spots occur with bridging and will be seen behind the withers. These typically are large areas, what I call the 'dove' area.

This is a very difficult area to be specific about. We are finding that there is no clinical data to support the common belief that dry spots cause injuries or are the result of excessive pressure to the back under the saddle. What we have found, over the years, is that where there is sweat this indicates pressure or contact on the back. If we find a Dry Spot it is from lack of pressure or contact and around the edges and one may get excessive pressure, which subsequently causes the white hair growth. Dry Spots are more often found up front behind the withers than over the loin of the back, where there is more motion between the saddle and the back. The saddle moves over the loin area more readily than in the front under the swells or pommel causing more friction and heat. Thus, one finds more 'blistering' over the loin area, but more hide and hair is worn off from direct pressure up front.

Fistulas, caused from direct pressure on the vertebrae at the withers, are a dangerous injury and will take close to a year to heal. Be cautious that the gullet does not rest on the blankets or pads over the withers.

CAUSES

Poor fit is the main cause. Other factors maybe: the horse is larger on one side than the other, or the horse is not fit. Horses that are 'soft' and not fit tend to sore-up when first ridden, blankets that wrinkle behind the withers, blankets that fill up the 'tunnel' between the skirts or panels, synthetic blankets that do not 'wick-away' the sweat and cause over heating will all cause soreness.

Wool blankets and old fashion wool or horse hair blankets are best. The wool blankets can be shaped to stop wrinkles and absorb sweat better than the synthetics.

USING THE SWEAT METHOD TO TEST FIT

Looking for sweat areas, as described above, is not full proof because of possible excessive pressure points around the withers. But if one palpates the areas with the fingers (checks for soreness) in the sweat areas these can be detected whether dry or wet. If sore or tender, then the fit is incorrect and the saddle fit must be adjusted.

SADDLE FITTING IS NOT EASY - BUT IT PAYS OFF

PALPATING THE BACK
Look for soreness with your fingers

Palpating the back before saddling and after unsaddling is good management. Use your fingers.

NEW INJURIES
Injuries come from poor fit. You cannot pad out poor fit. Excess concentrations of pressure are going to cause injury to the back.

Right after the saddle comes off you may only see a different direction the hair is laying - but no puffiness from fluid blisters. This may or may not be sore. Test these areas with the ends of your fingers - like testing a cake. The horse may or may not drop away or 'flinch' from pain - but 'hood' its eyes, turn its ears back, turn its head back to you, flip its lower lip, step away, or crank its tail - you have to carefully watch and know your horse when it shows pain.

Wait about 20 minutes and look over the back again, by this time fluid will have time to accumulate in the injured areas. It may be only as thick as a paperback cover right under the skin, but you can feel it. Feel the skin over the rump or neck then go back and try again, you will feel a mushy character to the injured areas. There is a 'tight facia' ligament covering the muscle in the back and it is pulled very tight, the fluid will be very 'spongy' compared to this. Test all the areas contacted by the bars or panels.

Make it a habit to run your fingers, or walk your fingers, over the back as you turn the horse out and when saddling the next day check it quickly again.

Put cold water or compresses on these areas to stop accumulation of fluid.

These blister areas, or 'sheet' blister areas, will probably go away in about 3 days, but if bruised again they will come back. If this continues <u>successfully</u> 3 or 4 times, they will become permanent injuries.

OLD INJURIES
Continued use on old injuries makes a permanent injury and may render the horse 'unridable'.

LOOK FOR A NEW SADDLE, NOT A NEW PAD.

Old injuries may or may not have fluid build-up, but they will most likely have the hair standing-up. If you get down and look across the back you can see the hair is courser/dry and 'hooped' up as compared to the healthy hair around it. They will usually indicate soreness with the fingers. Near the bottom of these old sites it may have white hair. They have been abused for a long time. These sites may not get sore until the back 'cools' some and is 'cold', like the next morning. Checking 'cold' backs is good horsemanship. The horse has to be rested until the back is 'sound' and a proper fitting saddle found.

SADDLE SORES

Some horses 'warm' up and out of signs of back soreness. Do not accept this as a cure to the problem. Treat it like you would like to be treated yourself.

The horse will exhibit behavior or travel in a different way if he has a sore back. Such things as traveling with a 'hollow' back and the head and neck are higher than usual, or there is a hollow behind the withers that is sort of unusual. Only you, as the one who really knows the horse, can read these signs quickly. If you have chronic soreness, other muscle groups will get sore, counteracting the sore areas, and these you can feel with your fingers. There are 4 areas that usually get sore right along with the back: down the back of the scapula to the elbow, just above the shoulder at the base of the neck, the neck muscles behind the ears, and/or over the rump on either side of the tail. These can be telltale signs of deep back muscle soreness that is on the chronic side.

DEEP MUSCLE INJURIES

Deep muscle injuries are harder to locate and you will have to press much harder and longer with your fingers to locate these sites or injuries. Press down along the sides of the backbone following the deep muscles and down and over the withers, wherever the bars make contact. Press for 10 or 15 seconds in these areas with a strong steady pressure. If the horse reacts beyond his first initial response, because he does not know what you want or are doing, and dips his back, or steps away, or throws his head towards you, etc., you have a deep muscle injury. In addition, you have a saddle that is not fitting.

The cure is the same; rest and a saddle that fits.

THE BACKBONE

Always check the top of the backbone under the saddle area. The top of these vertebrae can often be bruised by making contact with each other, or by pressure, and be injured. Immediate relief from the saddle is a must, next anti-inflammatories can be used along with a prolonged rest. The saddle cannot touch the backbone in any place and this must be corrected.

MAKE ROOM FOR THE SCAPULA

When saddling, be very careful to place the saddle a good 2 inches behind the cartilage that sits on top of the scapula. I call it the 'scapula hook', where the scapula and the cartilage connect. The scapula travels back from the standing position, a good 2 to 3 inches, on most horses, when the legs are extended forwards.

Be very careful not to get the saddle too forward so the scapula hits the bars of the saddle.

BLANKET TIPS

Pads compressed in the gullet may raise the saddle causing bridging.

Blankets should not compress over the spine. So make sure there is ample room for the pads/blankets to fit between the skirts. Too narrow a gullet or throat will cause compression and overheating...overheating must be avoided.

The spread and height of the gullet/throat may not fit over the thick pads, pinching the withers. The excessive pinching causes heat and eventual soreness.

A good rule of thumb is to allow 1/2" to 3/4" extra width in the gullet/throat to allow for the width of the pads/blankets. In addition, the gullet/throat should not ride down on the top of the withers, but clear the top vertebrae by at least 2-1/2" to 3" in height.

More pads, more slipping.

Contour pads with fabric ridge.

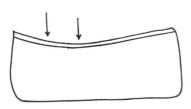

It is generally a wise practice to not use too many thick pads/blankets under the saddle, even if you are roping. A good choice seems to put on one good blanket to absorb the sweat and then a pad. Extra pads make the saddle slip around, but the saddle bars must still fit the back. Extra pads will not correct a poor fit.

Sculptured and sewn down the middle pads and contoured pads are really the best. These pads and/or blankets will fit down behind the withers without wrinkling.

Overheating is the main culprit with pads/blankets. Areas that do not cool down when sweaty, overheat and cause damage. Old horsehair pads, felt pads, and wool blankets still seem to be the best. The wool blankets 'wick' away the sweat and this keeps the back cool. This natural material works better than the synthetics.

UNEVEN BACKS

Horses and mules occasionally are bigger on one side than the other and a brief examination of this is necessary with new animals.

OLD INJURIES

Old wounds and scar tissue need to be given relief so that the tissue is not injured. 'Sculpting or skiving' the pads works good for this.

SADDLING SOFT HORSES

A long or hard ride on a 'soft' horse (one that is out of shape) is going to cause soreness. Once the horse is in 'shape' or 'fit', the same saddle and pads may not fit. The back will change shape as the horse hardens and becomes fit. It is always wise management to gradually increase your workouts allowing for the horse to gain shape, with a final check to ensure a good saddle fit. It may require two saddles.

BENDABLE SADDLE TREES

A California firm produces a flexible polymer tree, to your specifications, that flexes with the horse's back. It also will accommodate different horse's backs. It can be built to different strengths to be used for roping, ranch work, endurance, training, or pleasure.

ADD-ONS TO THE TREE TO STOP BRIDGING.

The idea of using a pad to attach to the bottom of the tree is good, if the pad is firm enough, like leather, so as to not allow point loading (the golf ball under the mattress idea) to occur. If it is 'skived' to fit the 'swale' so it tapers on the edges - and is secured to the tree - it will work. The above manufacturer also manufactures Velcro (R) attached-pads that stick to the bottom of the panels or tree. Leather can also be used and I have made this work successfully for some of my fitting problems.

PADS UNDER THE BLANKET OR SADDLE PAD.

Pads under the saddle blanket or saddle pad leave edges that cause soreness. Those that are tapered, if properly located, make a minor improvement. Fitting the tree is by far the best way to solve a fitting problem. Basically, you cannot pad out a poor fitting tree. You need another saddle.

LEVEL RIDE SADDLES WITH THE STIRRUPS WAY FORWARD.

The theory that initiated the moving of the stirrups forward was to put the weight down over the elbow of the horse. The leg is to act as a column and the horse can carry the weight best over the leg rather than in the middle of the back. Analogous to a suspension bridge.

We have tested this and unfortunately with placing the stirrups forward puts the weight where the rider sits and that is - in the majority of cases - on the back of the saddle. This appears to be because the rider cannot put significant weight into the stirrups to lift the body off the saddle as they ride. The legs seem to push the rider back into the cantle. When I was a boy, the ranchers called that 'cantle pounding' and they disliked anyone that rode this way because it made the horse's back sore over the loin.

LOCATING THE SEAT IN THE MIDDLE OF THE SADDLE SO THE LEG IS IN THE GROOVE OR CREASE.

In addition, the stirrups in the forward position are to help locate the leg in the crease between the barrel and the shoulder where it is narrower.

If the seat is moved forward to the middle of the saddle, this feature can be retained. If the seat is back and the stirrups are moved back, then one has to grip the horse where the body is wider.

BALANCE RIDE	The theory behind putting the stirrups far forward on a saddle is to concentrate the weight of the rider over the column of the leg, like the bareback seat. When the seat is back, the rider maybe 6" to 10" behind the bareback position and loading their weight on the deep back, not over the leg. This can be demonstrated with - weight testing.
STIRRUP POSITION IN RELATIONSHIP TO THE CENTER OF THE SEAT.	As it has been stated many times in this book that the stirrups seem best when placed 5" or 6" ahead of the low spot in the seat and this 5" or 6" should be placed in the center of the saddle bars. This way the rider's weight is evenly distributed over the entire surface of the face of the bars.
ANOTHER FACTOR The inside of the leg gives you a better grip.	Another factor associated with this stirrup and seat placement is its effect on the riding skill. When a rider is in the chair seat position, the rider is gripping more with the back of the leg and knee than the inside of the leg, the leg is bent and does not have the gripping power as a straighter leg. In addition, the leg is pushed forward and it cannot put as much weight in the stirrups and get the heels below the toes.
A FACT	Getting the weight over the bareback position, or relatively close as is practical, is important to the design/function of a saddle.

SADDLE
CONFORMATION
STEPS

1) Locate the bars 2" behind the scapula hook to the 'bow' of the last rib.

2) Place bars in this position on the back.

3) Locate the cinch line 3" or so behind the elbow or the 'flat' spot of the barrel.

4) Locate the seat center plus 5" or 6" in the center of the bars.

5) Locate the stirrup line 5" or 6" ahead of the center of the seat.

6) Set the location and style of the forks and cantle (Western) or pommel and cantle (English) to your preference.

FORWARD OR DEEP SEATED SADDLES	This is a controversial subject with most horsemen; using the deep seat or the forward seat.
	I, personally, only want the two following reasons addressed:
THE MAIN ISSUES	1) Which seat gives the horse the most distribution of weight over the entire bars and is easiest on the back. 2) Which seat makes the rider ride better.
ITEM (1) 	This is like facing Pikes Peak in worn out tennis shoes - because so much of the market is in favor of the 'most comfortable', 'deep seat'.
	But in using the White Pad Testing Method, described in this book, or measuring the weight shift of 'Deep Seat' versus the 'Stand Up Seat', as I call it, in the middle of the bars, it is superior to the Deep Seat. The Deep Seat concentrates the weight invariably under the cantle in an area about the size of your hand - one on each side of the spine, despite how far forward or back the stirrups are located.
ITEM (2) In the correct position, if the stool is removed, the rider remains standing.	In observing the most successful riders, a majority seem to come forward over their stirrup-line and achieve a standing-seat, as I call it. This happens when the feet and legs support the torso's weight and balance. This is not possible with the chair seat and better riders come forward, even in deep seat saddles, to achieve this position. In the chair seat the torso is controlled by the anatomy supporting the seat of the pants.
THE CENTER-SEAT OR STAND-UP SEAT 	All the major cavalries in the mid-1800's went to nearly forward or balanced ride saddles, as well as early American saddles and things did not change until the 40's and 50's. Historical evidence seems to point towards this forward or center-seat position as the better for the horse and rider.
	I have owned or trained somewhere over a 1,000 head of horses and from my own experience, I have ridden in both types - stock saddles and English saddles - and I do a better job and the horses do better when I ride the Center Seat Saddles. I ride forward behind the withers and control my weight with the support of my lower legs under me.
FREE SWINGING STIRRUPS	If you are going to ride broncy horses, you need your stirrups to be 'free-swinging' so you can get your feet forward to catch your weight.

OTHER USES

There are specialty uses for saddles, such as jumping and its related events, or bronc riding and its related events, or cutting, that one can use saddles with the stirrups hung farther forward.

HORSE COMFORT

Getting the horse comfortable is by far the most important factor in the saddle equation. But that cannot happen without the proper fit and a rider that sits in the proper seat.

A rider's weight is multiplied something like 2 to 3 times with each 'bounce' or post. Thus, fit becomes vital - through weight ditribution over the saddle tree.

RIDE LIGHT - DON'T BUMP

BARS MUST FIT THE WITHERS POCKET

SWELLS, GULLET, POMMEL, OR FORKS CONTROL THE FIT. WESTERN OR ENGLISH

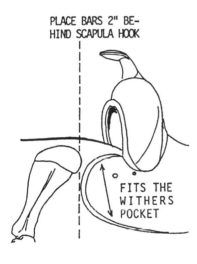

PLACE BARS 2" BE-HIND SCAPULA HOOK

FITS THE WITHERS POCKET

SADDLE SITS TOO HIGH, SWELLS TOO NARROW, SADDLE TIPS BACK.

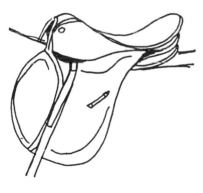

GULLET, TUNNEL, OR THROAT TOO NARROW. SITS TOO HIGH. SADDLE TIPS BACK, NOT LEVEL.

The front end on many saddles, both Western and English, are not wide enough or deep enough to come down over the withers and fit into the 'pocket' alongside the back of the withers. On Western saddles, the shape of the bars on the front end of the saddle are not crafted properly to fit into this concave area comfortably. Many of them are too small and rounded rather than larger and a little flatter to make a comfortable fit into this depression. The result is after the saddle has been on the back for a while - it slowly starts to get sore in this area. The horse starts walking stiff legged on the front end and may even buck or shy on subsequent rides.

Front ends of saddles that do not fit often times drop the saddle down and back or tilt it up in front. Getting the saddle up to 2" behind the scapula hook places the saddle so the pocket of the saddle is far enough forward. Most saddles move the stirrups forward to accomplish this because the low spot or pocket is too far back on the horse. It is very important that the saddle fits in this area, to locate it on the back correctly.

The influence of the 'flat back' Quarter Horse has caused a great demand for this type of saddle. The bars on many of these saddles do not drop down far enough on the sides of the horse to accommodate a horse with a taller vertebrae. Many of the early saddles, built for smaller horses, were too narrow for this type of horse. But in the late 30's and 40's saddles built for the working cowboy and discriminating horseman saw the throats on the old style saddles open up. These are your Stand-Up-Seat Saddles: The Louellen, Association, Visalia, Roper, Low Moose, Will James, and Plainsman. But with the onslaught of the show horse with flat backs, straight shoulders, straight pasterns and small feet, in came the flat fronted high riding bars. These bars ride too high on the front end of the horse, tilting many of these saddles back, especially with a horse with withers. If the bars drop into the saucer area behind the withers properly, the saddle will sit flatter along the top line.

Straight shoulders have a tendency to have less distance between the top of the scapula cartilage and the top of the vertebrae lifting the front of the saddle.

59

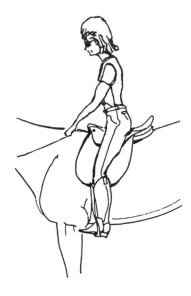

BRIDGING

RIDER'S WEIGHT

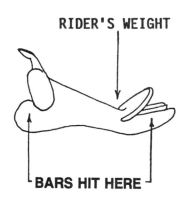

BARS HIT HERE

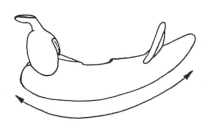

If the seat or pocket is moved forward and the saddle is flatter or lower in the middle - this puts the legs in the crease where the rider can still get his legs and feet under the upper 60% of his weight or torso. If he sits back, because the stirrups are placed over the crease and the seat moved back, he cannot get into a balanced seat.

So the discriminating horseman must be very selective with the purchase of a saddle. Get one that puts you forward enough to get your legs in the crease and the low spot is in the middle of the saddle where you can get your weight over your legs.

Start by a careful inspection of the shoulder and withers so you can pick out the proper pommel or swells for your saddle selection.

An improper fit up front over the withers may also cause bridging from the withers to the small of the back. This is a low level pain at first, but it grows into a substantial pain as time goes by.

This defect introduces bridging, where the saddle does not fit down into the swale behind the withers and with your added weight it puts a great load per square inch in the small of the back. The pressure winds up being concentrated in an area smaller than the palm of your hand. Higher withered horses tend to have more curve in this area and so they are easier to sore up. Quarter Horse saddles fit Quarter Horses with flatter, straighter backs, but will not fit most working or running Quarter Horses or many other higher withered breeds. Be aware of this and look into this bridging very carefully before buying.

If the saddle fits the shoulder and the saddle still bridges it maybe because the saddle curls up too much in the back under the cantle. Concentrating all the rider's weight right under the cantle.

Or, the bars maybe just too straight and this still causes the concentration of weight in two small areas on the back under the rider.

If the seat is near the middle of the saddle and with the stirrups 5" to 6" a head of the center spot of the seat or pocket - the saddle maybe worth investing in having strips of leather glued to the bottom of the bars. This is done in successive layers and then shaped with a horse file to fit the back. This can be done by your saddlemaker with the help of your horse.

RESHAPING THE BARS

Take the skirts off the saddle - get some Barge glue and an old horse rasp from your farrier - and go to fitting the bars to the horse's back.

SEAL THE PARTS WHERE YOU RASP THROUGH THE 'HIDE' OF THE TREE WITH A GOOD SEALER. This prevents the wood from drying out

You can add leather strips in successive layers to the bottom of the bars and then rasp them to fit the horse's back. Layers that are about 1/8" thick work best.

Lift the saddle from both ends to see if it is fitting down the curve of the back behind the withers as well as sloping properly with the back so it is not 'raftering'. If it tips down too far, it pinches the sides of the back - if it tips out too far, it 'flops' down on the top of the back. You cannot fix this.

Then replace the skirts, but wet the leather first, and then cinch it down to a good fit and let it dry. Now try it out with some long rides on the horse. Finger the horse's back, as shown, afterwards to see if you have done a good job or use the White Pad Method.

Always check the horse's back after each ride. All the old master horsemen I saw, who made a living a horse-back, checked the back after unsaddling. Then before saddling, when the back was cold, would check it again.

CHECK AND MAKE SURE YOU HAVE ONE PIECE SKIRTS.

If you have spliced-together-skirts rather than all one piece skirts, the overlaps or bridges will still hurt the back even if the tree fits. I would not attempt to refit the bars to the back unless I had all-one-piece-skirts. Good saddlemakers generally do not make spliced skirts and they should be near 1/4" thick to spread the weight.

BOTTOM OF TREE SHOWS LATIGO LEATHER PATCHES

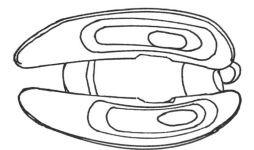

BUILT UP STRIPS OF LEATHER ARE GLUED ON WITH BARGE GLUE, THEN RASPED OFF TO REMOVE THE EDGES AND SHAPE THE BARS TO FIT THE HORSE'S BACK.

If the skirts are connected behind the cantle be sure they do not ride on the backbone as it may cause soreness. If the 'Jockey' is sewn on top of the skirts it is less likely to touch the backbone.

WESTERN SADDLE TREES

Selecting a tree 'uncovered' is the best route to take when purchasing a new saddle. This, of course, is the most expensive approach because custom saddles do not come cheap. But being able to 'see' that tree sitting flat on the horse's bare back will allow you the best fit. Or, if you need modifications you can see how to make those changes to the bars.

DIFFERENCES IN TREES YOU SHOULD UNDERSTAND Working saddles are covered with Bullhide or Rawhide. They shrink as they dry and make the tree very strong.

RAWHIDE OR BULLHIDE

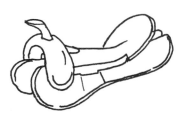

SYNTHETIC TREES HAVE THE SEAT BUILT IN.

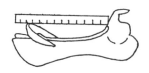

MEASURING A WESTERN SADDLE

Bullhide and Rawhide Trees Offer:

1) Wood carved, Bullhide or Rawhide trees are the strongest and capable of roping, ranch work, or training facility.
2) They are capable of being repaired, or the bars re-sculptured.
3) They are heavier and more expensive than plastic trees.
4) They offer a good variety of selection.
5) They have longevity and hold their value longer.
6) You can custom style the ground seat.
7) You can change the position of the stirrups.
8) The stirrups can be made to swing free.

Synthetic, Plastic, Ralide Trees for Pleasure Saddles

1) Not made for heavy use. No roping, training, packing in the mountains, or ranch work.
2) Not easily repaired - better to replace the saddle.
3) Lighter than Rawhide and less expensive.
4) A smaller selection than their counter parts, especially in the Stand-Up-Seat saddles.
5) Plastic trees do not hold their value and make the saddle a little harder to resell.
6) You cannot custom fit the ground seat because it is precast in the molding process right with the tree. It is part of the tree. You only get what the manufacturer has to offer.
7) You cannot change the position of the stirrup leathers (no forward or backward adjusting) because there is only one channel to guide the leathers through and over the bars. You are subject to just what the manufacturer has to offer.
8) The stirrups cannot be 'unplugged' to allow for free swinging stirrups. The stirrup leathers mounting channel, mentioned above, between the bars and the ground seat, does not allow for remodeling. You cannot get at it to work on it. The majority of these saddles could use freer swinging stirrups to be <u>safe</u>.

TREE STYLES

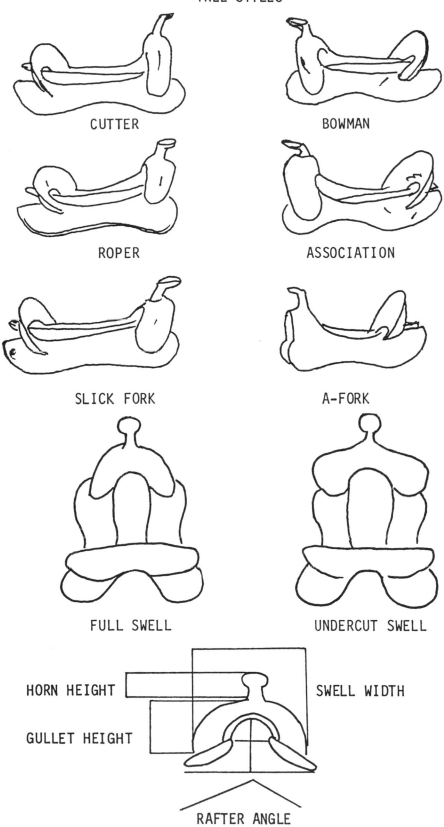

CUTTER

BOWMAN

ROPER

ASSOCIATION

SLICK FORK

A-FORK

FULL SWELL

UNDERCUT SWELL

HORN HEIGHT

SWELL WIDTH

GULLET HEIGHT

RAFTER ANGLE

A-FRAME AND SLICK FORK SADDLES

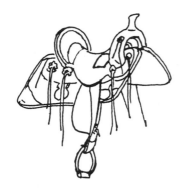

A-FRAME

A-Frame Saddle is an old name for Slick Fork - high front end saddles. Many old time saddles were built this way. Before the Quarter Horse influence, with flatter, broader withers, there were many more smaller, narrower backed, higher withered horses on the market. Thus, this type of saddle was popular. It also provides a narrower waist or plate making long distant riding more comfortable. It also fits the withers-pocket a little deeper and keeps the saddle a little flatter. These saddles are open between the plate and the swells giving a good hand hold for carrying and also a good entry for additional air into the underside of the saddle for cooling. Many were rigged with a double cinch usually full-double or 7/8ths.

The stirrups were hung at the center of the saddle or slightly forward. The swells tilt forward along with a wide tilt forward horn that has a large cap. The large cap helps with a fast running rope so the dallies do not come off.

Many were high-backed and this is not as popular today. The average height today is 4" to 3-1/2" because riders today are not handling range horses like many riders were faced with in the past. If the cantle is cut down these saddles are very functional for today's riding requirements. Discriminating riders today are going back to these older styles that have proven to be very functional for athletic riding and long distance riding as well as easier to fit the horse's back.

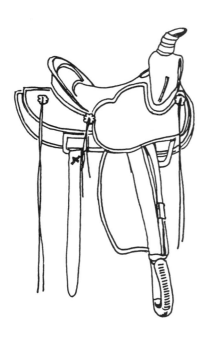

SLICK FORK

The centered riding position of the rider over the middle of the saddle and the deep bow of the bars make this saddle comfortable on the horse's back. These features are in much higher demand today as competition in all events is causing horsemen to seek out better and more workable techniques to improve their performance. Ranchers and trainers have always used them throughout the years, but it has been more the recreational market that has made deep seat saddles popular after the Second World War. Tree designs such as: Association, Louellen, Visalia, Will James, Low Moose Roper, and Roper saddles reflect the A-Frame design and are still seen in ranch country throughout western United States.

Unfortunately, most of the original A-Frame saddles are too narrow to be used on today's horses.

SADDLE CHOICES

CHOICES IN BARS

AR Arabian Bars
AZ Arizona Bars
NZ New Arizona Bars
NW Northwest Bars
QH Quarter Horse Bars
SQ Semi-Quarter Horse Bars

GIRTH/CINCH RIGGING SELECTIONS. THE COMMON WAY THE TUGS GO OVER THE TREE.

7/8 to Full Double with double D's or all in the skirt
5/8 to Full double with double D's or all in the skirt
3-Way rigging in the skirt
Flat plate rigging
Dropped D
Full single, 5/8, 7/8 with tugs that connect or go over the tree.

SWELLS

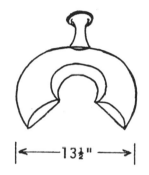

|←——13½"——→|

(A-frame or under cuts)
Slick Fork saddles no swells
Swells (By the inch range from 9-1/2" to 13-1/2" wide)

Slick forks are less apt to hurt you in case the horse falls, are less tiring to ride over long distances because of the narrower waist, and can be used with bucking rolls to stop going over the front of the saddle. Same as swells, but less likely to cause injury.

Solid Swells give a place to lock your thighs under to hold yourself on if the horse jumps, stumbles, bucks, etc. Better for riding green stock than slick forks for the average rider. Most saddles have some swells.

HORNS

(A) Short Post and Heavy Duty
(B) Tall Dally Posts and range from 1-3/4" to 3-1/2"
(C) Cap type
(D) Cutter Horn

(A)   (B)   (C)   (D)

CHEYENNE ROLLS

Are preferred by many because of the extra handhold it offers in emergencies, and they do look good.

CANTLE HEIGHTS

Range: 3-1/2" to 5" with 3-1/2" the most common height

GULLET SIZE

Horizontal width range: 6" to 9" with 7" most common.
Vertical height range: 6" to 6-3/4" with 6-1/2" common.

TREE LENGTH SEAT SIZE

Seat size, from swells to cantle, range 13" to 18" with seat sizes 15" to 16" the most common.

SKIRTS

Skirts come in small, large, or square.

BARS

Arizona Bars
Practically the same as a standard bar, except on the underside of the bar for the front side of the stirrup leather cutout it is thicker. Recommended for heavier uses.
Features Standard Rocker, Rafter and Twist.

New Arizona Bars
Practically the same.

Northwest Bars
A cross between a standard and Hercules tree; essentially that it has more Rocker effect.
Features More Rocker, Standard Rafter, More Twist.

Arabian Bars
Same as a standard bar, but cut off behind the cantle to make them shorter.

Semi-Quarter Horse
Narrower throat than Full Quarter Horse Bars.
Features Standard Rocker, Rafter, and Twist.

Full Quarter Horse
Front bar in throat: Top: 6-1/2 inches wide or wider.
Bottom: 13 inches or more wider.
Features Standard Rocker, Flatter Rafter, and Standard Twist.

TREES FEATURE
THESE OPTIONS:
1) Style
2) Cantle height
3) Swells width and height
4) Throat width
5) Type of bars (Rocker, Rafter, Twist)
6) Type of tree (Bullhide, Rawhide, Plastic)
7) Saddle tree design
8) Seat style on some (Narrow waist, flat seat)

Custom Saddles
Generally, custom saddles are two times more expensive than factory production style saddles, but more than worth the expense because they are built to fit the horse, fit the rider, and will last more than two times the life of a catalog saddle.

Tooling
Tooling is extra - a cosmetic amenity, but certainly it enhances your pride of ownership.

ADJUSTABLE CINCH "D"s
LOCATION OF GIRTHS
AND CINCHAS

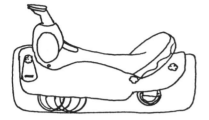

The cinch rings should be located approximately 3" off the elbow and up 3" to an area that is predominately flat. This is an ideal location because it lessens the risk of galling the side of the horse when it is 'cinched' up.

The front cinch will be properly located approximately 3" behind the elbow and crossing the brisket near the middle. Too far forward may catch the webbing of the forearm. It is important that the cinch holds the saddle in its proper place between the 'scapula hook' and the 'curve of the last rib'. The 'D' rings must coordinate with the cinch location. Multiple locations of the 'D's is very helpful so that the cinch locations are correct on different horses.

The back cinch is usually about 12" to 16" back and should be equipped with a keeper-strap to connect it to the front cinch ring. It is most important to have them connected to stop the back cinch from flopping back. If it is loose, it can swing back by the flanks where it is loose enough to catch a hind foot in case of a spill. This can spell real trouble.

IT HELPS THE SADDLE
FIT IF THE BACK
CINCH IS CINCHED-UP

ADJUSTABLE IN-SKIRT
RIGGING

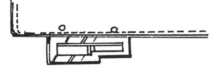

STRAP OVER TREE
RIGGING

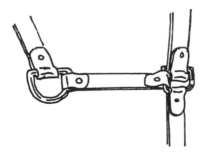

IN PLATE OVER THE
TREE RIGGING

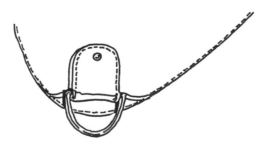

SADDLE HORNS

SHORT POST, HEAVY DUTY, TALL DALLY POSTS OR CAP TYPES (AVERAGE 2-5/8" WIDE).CUTTER HORNS (4-1/2" HIGH BY 1-1/4" WIDE).

The saddle horn needs to have a secure cap cover because if the metal is exposed 'ever' it becomes a cutting tool. Make sure the cap is secured and protective. In addition, too tall and too small are both dangerous in that the horn can get under your coat or vest and keep you out of the seat. This spooks your horse and you can get bucked off. Too small on top can penetrate your stomach in a wreck - larger is safer. Too far back is also dangerous for this same reason. Forward placed with a larger horn is safer. Dally roper horns are too high for average riding, and cutter horns are dangerous.

Horns can be ordered by height and slope; 3" to 5" is common. Forward or straight up for heeling dallies is better.

BLEVINS POSITION

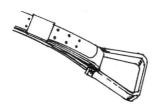

If you are using Blevins on your stirrup leathers they should be placed below your knee position 3" to 4" so they do not rub on any of the leather on the skirt or cinch latigos. Gradual wear develops sharp edges on the Blevins and consequently they cut away the leather they rub against. This can be expensive. Some are covered with leather and this helps as long as you keep them well covered.

NAILS IN THE THROAT OF THE SADDLE

English and Western saddles have many nails in the throat of the gullet holding the pommel parts together tucked backup on the underside. Check these out continually for they have a habit of working loose. The nails and screws on the lower side of the forks or pommel are the worst offenders and need constant checking. These can hurt the horse and are often overlooked buried in the sheepskin of the skirts. Automatically run your hand in this area each time you use the saddle to feel for loose nails or screws.

THE LACINGS

Check the lacings to make sure they go under the surface of the sheepskin or they can rub sore spots on the horse's back.

CRAWLING SHEEPSKIN

Some new synthetic materials for the skirts and sheepkin itself can 'crawl' or 'creep' with the motion of the horse. Because the 'lean' of the hairs has to face each other on both skirts. With sheepskin they rotate one of the hides so it faces the other properly. Your saddlemaker can instruct you here. I like it so it pulls down on both sides - not lifting or crawling. Observe your saddle in use and see if it crawls or 'draws' the blankets on one side into wrinkles. This indicates the sheepskin in facing the wrong way on the skirt.

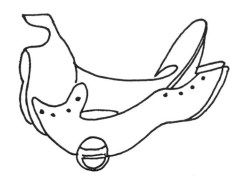

SINGLE FLAT PLATE

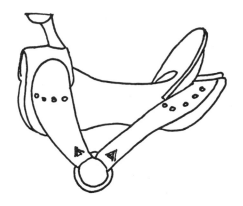

5/8 SINGLE STRAP

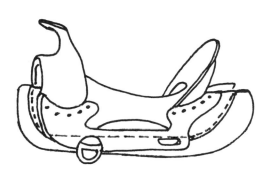

3/4 RIG IN SKIRT WITH
UNDER PLATE IN TREE

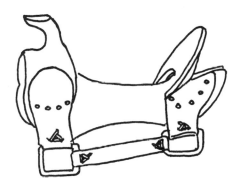

FULL DOUBLE IN TREE

Study the back, withers, and elbow
and they will tell you what style
and placement of rigging to use.

DOUBLE OR SINGLE CINCHAS

If you are rigged forward and do any training, roping, or riding in the hills, use the second cinch 'snugged' up.

This rigging is always helped with the use of a breast collar.

Full double, 7/8 and 3/4 rigged saddles are pulled down forwards by the cinch and the back of the saddle rides up. When the rider gets on, the saddle leverages the soft muscles down, under the front of the saddle, like a pump handle. The second cinch helps, or 'pulls down', the saddle in back. This is true with both Western and English saddles. An over-girth is used on English saddles to overcome this effect. Whenever the rider bounces, or rides up in the stirrups like posting, the saddle comes back-up...and, eventually, sores up the muscles under the front of the saddle.

The second cinch is always needed with these forward rigged saddles and it needs to be drawn-up snug. It also needs the keeper to connect it to the forward cinch, so, in case of a spill, a hind leg cannot get caught-up and cause a serious wreck.

3/4 and 5/8

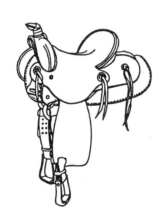

If your horse calls for a 3/4 or 5/8 rigged outfit, you will find these saddles are helped by plate or single rigging. These saddles stay forward caused by the position of the cinch that is more in the middle of the saddle. Too often, however, this position, if not calculated correctly, will help the saddle bridge between the withers and the loin. This needs to be check.

If you are riding hard and fast in rough country, training, or roping give some thought to still using a second cinch. The second cinch, with the 3/4 and 5/8, will still help stop the 'pull down' effect by the cinch on the forward portion of the saddle and when roping you will find it keeps the saddle better anchored.

Saddling bucking horses and colts

The 3/4, 5/8 and center fire rigging work well to hold the saddle forward in the 'action' closer to the middle of the 'teeter totter' - away from the thrust of the back coming up when the horse fires. Plus, if a second cinch is used, it holds the back of the saddle down so it does not 'tip' forward so far, popping your legs off the swells.

It all boils down to good fit, but if you push down on the cantle and it feels a bit springy, I would use a second cinch.

TWISTED SADDLES

CINCH "D's" and BILLETS not lined up.

Cinchas and billets that are incorrectly placed on the saddle can pull the saddle out of position. Also, if the Cinch D's or billets are not in equal positions on both sides of the saddle, they can make the saddle 'twist' or 'crawl' to one side and make the horse sore.

This is also true with the stirrup leathers and, of course, the tree.

Measure from the front of the saddle horn or pommel back to the D's and stirrup leathers and check this out.

If the stirrups are not the same length, the saddle will also crawl.

Many factory trees are twisted and do not 'measure' up to even on both sides.

LOCATING THE CINCH D's OR BILLETS ON A SADDLE.

Different types of horse's backs will place the cinch D's or billets in different locations. And, it is best not to generalize this and say, "Oh well!, because this is a Semi-Quarter horse it will take a 7/8 or 3/4 rigging." Because so often, depending on the breeding, that horse may have real deep withers or it may not. It maybe very flat and with a straight shoulder - yet, still a Semi-Quarter horse style. So, it pays to go through the basic exercise of locating the D's or billets, as described below.

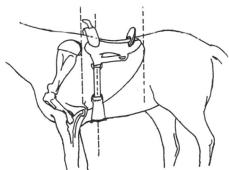

STEP ONE

Locate the heart-flat-spot 3" behind the horse's elbow and about 3" up (roughly the width of your hand). This is where the cinch rings should locate on this flat spot. On this flat spot it is less likely to gall-up a horse and it is right over the brisket and back far enough not to catch the webbing of the legs. Farther back includes more of the stomach muscle that does not have bone to support it and this can bother a horse.

71

Properly locating the bars and the cinch will make the saddle stay put.

Place the saddle on the horse's back with the front of the bars 2" behind the scapula hook (a bump on the back side of the top of the scapula) and to the curve of the last rib, (straight out off the backbone about 8"). The bars should fit in this location to fit properly.

Now, bring a line up from the cinch rings (on the flat spot on the side of the horse's elbow) and locate it on the saddle bars. This locates the proper position for the center of the saddle D's or billets.

There is no variable, this is exact, not kinda here will do. Wherever it lands is the proper location. If the bars fit the back, the saddle will stay put.

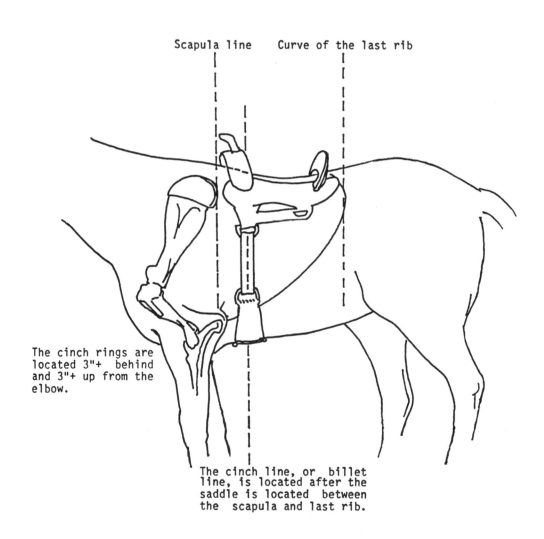

Scapula line   Curve of the last rib

The cinch rings are located 3"+ behind and 3"+ up from the elbow.

The cinch line, or billet line, is located after the saddle is located between the scapula and last rib.

SKIRTS

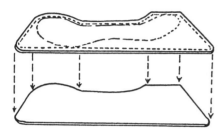

Thick skirts help
spread the weight

Skirts play a significant roll in spreading the weight
and in helping the bars work with the horse's back.
The stiffer the skirt material the less the physical
equation of 'point loading' works. This is the golf
ball under the mattress concept. Thick stiff skirts
help the bars transfer the weight and spread it out
more evenly away from a 'point loading area' than
will thick pads of any kind.

I have seen this work on saddles that were almost a
fit, to add another layer of skirting leather to the
existing skirts. This makes the skirts a good 3/8"
thick (two 12 or 13 ounce pieces of oak tanned skirting
leather) glued and stitched together. Then skive the
edges front and back and under the cinch locations to
stop the edges from 'digging in'. Use good Barge glue
or contact cement. This can help endurance riders,
outfitters, and ropers, especially.

In Argentina it is common with the Goucho saddle to add
an extra piece of leather over the sheepskin pads, then
on goes the saddle. I have seen deer hides over heavy
wool or horsehair pads on problem soft backed horses.

Where the skirts end under the gullet and along the top
side of the bars - this should not create a hard edge
so as to cause a ridge. It should be skived back,
especially in the gullet, where it is nailed or screwed
back to the inside of the forks or gullet.

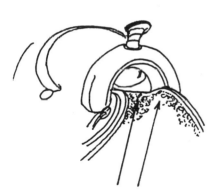

Make sure edges
are rounded off

Make sure the skirt stitching is in a groove and not
sitting on top of the leather. It wears out and gets
ripped off when it snags on things when done this way.

Use good sheepskin a good 3/4" thick that is oak tanned
for the underskirting. This is best.

Trees that fit into a skirt pocket only give you a one
layer thickness.

Keep saddles on a good stand so the skirts don't
curl-up, this hurts their effectiveness.

BREAST COLLARS
Straight leather
is best. Liners
get hard and sore
the horse up.

Breast collars hook onto the saddle on the skirt rings,
the billets on half-breeds, or the cinch D's. Use a
low position so you do not choke off the horse's wind.
Make sure the keeper to the cinch holds the breast
collar in a down position and won't let it ride up.

SKIRT STYLES   Skirts are made in a variety of designs. The important
things to consider are:

      Thickness
      All-one-piece
      Size and shape for your horse
      Quality lining

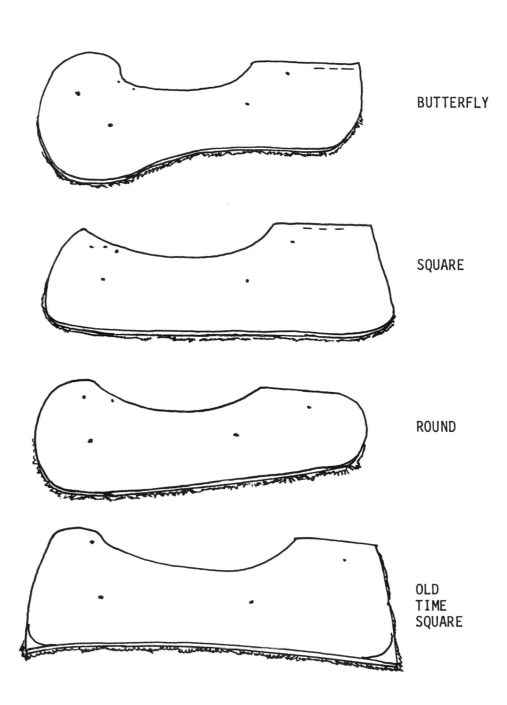

BUTTERFLY

SQUARE

ROUND

OLD
TIME
SQUARE

STIRRUP LEATHERS

Stirrup leathers suffer more wear and stress than any other part of the saddle. Inspect them carefully. A variety of styles are available - I would opt only for FULL LENGTH, one or two piece leathers. The quality of the leather is very important.

FULL LENGTH ONE PIECE

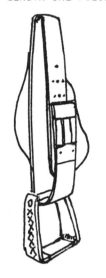

FULL LENGTH TWO PIECE

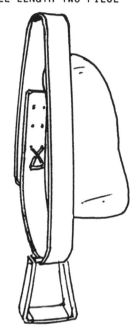

HALF LENGTH TWO PIECE

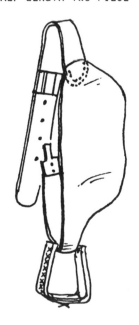

BUCKING ROLLS

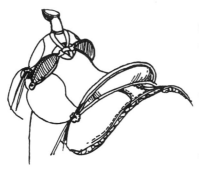

These are available through catalogs or saddle shops. They come in hard or soft. The size seems to be all about the same. They are designed to act as swells on Western saddles to keep you from being bucked off over the front of the horse.

I would get your saddlemaker to help you put these on because the placement is rather important. Bucking rolls are primarily used on 'slick fork' Western saddles. Make sure your installer has some experience in putting these on your saddle, because the screws that are used are quiet large and put big holes in the leather.

They also, 'in a form', are used on the front of Australian Stock Saddles for the same purpose.

LARIAT OR 'CATCH ROPE' KEEPERS THAT HOLD THE ROPE ON YOUR SADDLE

It is handier to have the keeper, or lace, higher up on the forks or swells nearer the horn. If the rope gets too low on the swells, you have the chance of putting your foot through the loops, and the higher loops do not beat up and down on your leg all day at the 'jangle'. The big thing is, however, it is much quicker and eaiser, when in a hurry, at the run, to get the rope off the saddle.

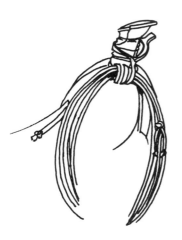

I have a loop in the end of the lace and hook it over the horn - but many times - unless you have a big horn cap - the lace slips off and you lose your rope.

The other way is to use a buckle - but then these are often hard to get undone with one hand - while at the run and trying to keep in position on a horse or cow.

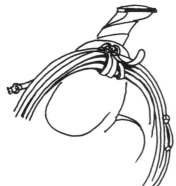

Your longer ranch ropes will stay on better with the buckle because you have a bigger bundle of rope. Also, the newer ropes are slicker and take more tension to hold in place than the older nylon or grass ropes. So, you are probably better off with the buckle set up just a couple inches below the horn on your throwing side. I have hung ropes behind the cantle, like the South Americans, but I seem to get tangled up in them, especially getting off and on the spooky ones.

THE SEAT

CONCAVE SHAPE AROUND WAIST OF SADDLE. A NARROW CROWN AND SEAT JOCKEY.

Called the waist, or crown, of the saddle this area is crucial to the comfort of the saddle and the rider's grip on the horse. A good grip locks you down deep into the saddle - no grip and you ride out or off the seat and behind the horse's moves - not with them. Watch riders in events like: working cow horse or cutting and you can see who is locked into the saddle and who is not. Some of this is attributable to the fit of the saddle to the rider in this grip area.

CROWN   SEAT
WAIST   POCKET

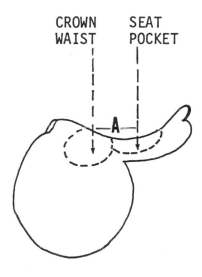

Two things are wrong with most pleasure saddles: (1) The area under your seat bones, 'the deep seat' of the saddle, is too round. It should be nearly flat. (2) The 'waist' or 'plate' just ahead of the deep seat is too wide. This transition from flat seat to narrow crest on the plate is started when the 'strainer plate' is put in - to form the 'seat'. Many saddles have too thick stirrup leathers, skirts, and seat jockey (the leather is too thick) and this makes the saddle too wide between the rider's thighs.

Wide hipped people can ride wider saddles, but they do not usually have round legs. Narrow hipped people, generally with round legs, will ride narrower saddles better. Wide saddles make your knees and toes point out and usually start hurting.

SEAT SLOPE
FLATTENING THE PLATE
Some saddles that are built-up too high in front of the pocket maybe worth lowering, or flattening, the top plate. If the pocket, or seat, is in the near center of the saddle and the stirrups are located 5" to 6" ahead of the low spot of the seat, then the investment of lowering this area maybe worth it.

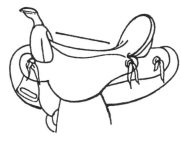

It is quite an enterprise. The conchas on either side of the swells must be taken off and an additional few screws taken out. Then the seat jockey can be folded back to expose the area for work. Sometimes removing a layer of leather may work, other times one can rasp this area down with a horse file and do a creditable job. The controlling factor is when the seat jockey is replaced; does it expose the nails and cuts on the bottom of the swells cover? This will not look good, so you need to limit your remodeling to this fact.

YOU CAN DO SEVERAL THINGS WITH THIS REMODEL.
(1) Make the pocket forward, or (2) flatten the crown to make a little more room to move forward and back, or (3) to 'narrow' the waist, or crown, for a better fit and grip. Narrow crowns ride better for most of us. The raised crown is comfortable to ride and if the seat is far enough forward it is not

a hinderence, but if it pushes the rider back out of the center...then it is. A flatter seat gives you more room to use additional cues not available with an equitation seat. One of the best examples is moving forward to free up the hinds for lead changes, etc.

CUPPED CANTLES

Cupped cantles on Western saddles versus flat ones are one's own preference. But I have found the slight cupping is more comfortable and gives a better seat. I know you do not slide out 'sideways' quite as easily as with a flatter cantle - for hard riding this is a plus.

THINNER STIRRUP LEATHERS AND FENDERS DO NOT HURT YOUR KNEES

Keeping the saddle thinner between the knees stops the hurting of the knees on longer rides.

Older style saddles had thinner stirrup leathers and fenders and the plate, or seat jockey, thinned out under the legs. This gave the rider a narrower and better fitting seat on the horse. This lighter leather also allowed the stirrups to swing forward and back easier. Riding the performance horse one needs the stirrups to be free swinging so you can keep your feet under your body when the horse makes athletic moves.

WHY WERE THEY THINNER?

Years ago saddlemakers had better leather to work with at reasonable prices and much of it was imported. Poorly tanned leather breaks too easily under stress, so today they have to use thicker leather. With quality leather you can have a narrower waisted saddle between your knees and free swinging stirrups - forward and back - but you have to pay the extra price.

ANOTHER WAY TO GET A NARROWER SADDLE Get a saddle that your legs go down the crease.

The wider saddle will wear the skin off behind your knees and make your knees hurt.

Narrower saddles come from sitting farther forward on the horse - because the legs are in the crease. Thinner saddles are much more comfortable to ride than wide saddles. The narrower ones also give us more leg grip on the horse. The wider your legs are apart, the less grip you have. Saddles that are narrower also make you ride better. There is no comparison between your ability to ride in a stand-up-seat - balanced over your legs - than in the sitting profile, or chair seat, on a horse. If the seat is forward, or in the middle of the saddle, the saddle will be narrower.

STICK YOUR STIRRUPS Helps the knees and ankles. Also, you can lace them backwards on one side if you know how.

Soak your stirrups in a tank for a few hours, then put a stick in them to rotate them into the 'riding' position and let them dry. This way it will take the pressure off your ankles, and give you a quicker 'pick-up' on the 'offside stirrup' when getting on. This can avoid a riding error that may save you an injury.

BARS ON THE DEEP BACK

CONVEX BARS FOR THE DEEP BACK

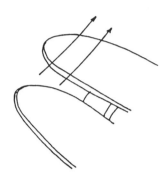

This is a supplimentary problem existing with the bridging from the withers to the small of the back, generally under the cantle. The back is gently convex or rounded out like the trunk lid of your car. The problem occurs because the bars are very often 'rounded out', or also convex, instead of slightly concave to fit this area.

Here we have the bars needing to be strongly convex to fit behind the withers and concave to conform to the convex shape of the deep or nearly flat back.

Not only is this a problem, but the raftering angle is very wide on the deep back in contrast to being quite narrow in the front. This is true for both English and Western saddles. This is called the 'twist' or flare.

This construction problem is a very common defect and compounds the bridging effect - or, by itself, will cause deep back soreness. To check this, stand the saddle up with the cantle down and sight down the tunnel between the skirts and look at the surface just below the cantle. If it is buldging out, usually in an area about the size of a saucer turned upside down, it will cause soreness. This is hard to correct without some expert refitting.

CORRECT RAFTER ANGLE

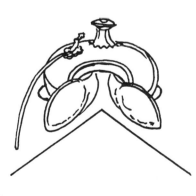

A few companies do build custom trees. However, most bars are massed produced and all the same. The bars make the fit - be selective.

The correct Raftering Angle in this area is also very critical. It can be best observed by putting the saddle on the horse and lifting the back of the saddle and comparing the angle of the skirts or bars with the sloping of the back. These must fit!

In addition, the bars must 'twist' from a narrow rafter angle for the withers to a very flat angle of the flat of the back. This cannot be corrected with blankets or refitting. You need a new saddle!

There are only a few major manufacturers of trees for Western saddles in the U.S. and they build for the largest share of the market - mostly one kind of back - and the bars all have primarily the same shape. It is the cantle and swells specifications that change along with the rafter angles. The bars generally have not changed to correspond with these specifications. Most are built from 2" x 6" stock rather than 3" x 7" or 4" x 7" material to meet the proper rocker, twist, or rafter and weight distribution requirements.

ENGLISH SADDLES

EVERYTHING GOES BETTER WITH THE RIGHT SADDLE. THE HORSE GOES BETTER AND THE RIDER RIDES BETTER.

English saddles with small bars or tube bars for a tree or cantle supports are unacceptable. Point loading occurs along the tube and cannot be overcome with padding or blankets.

In addition, the panel should be a good 6" to 8" wide on each side of the tunnel for proper weight distribution. Narrower than this is not wide enough under the cantle area. Most panels are too narrow to be off the backbone and only on the ribs.

Incorrect rafter angles are common in English saddles with the assumption that the panel padding will reposition itself and correct the difference. This is not so.

ENGLISH GULLET PLATE

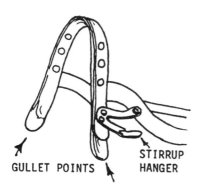

GULLET POINTS

STIRRUP HANGER

The Gullet Plate or forks on many English saddles is very often ill fitting. The shape looks like the illustration. The area marked with the arrows often digs into the side of the horse if too tight. The fit must be very carefully controlled; not too <u>loose</u> or too <u>tight</u>. The horse gets sore, shortens its stride, sometimes limps, or raises its neck high to alleviate the pain. Saddle selection is important to check this fit very carefully. The gullet plate points can be checked by placing the saddle in position and then feeling the 'points' with your fingers and estimate the amount of pressure. They should curve out slightly. The shoulder will expand a great deal at this point with movement.

SEAT PANEL NAILS

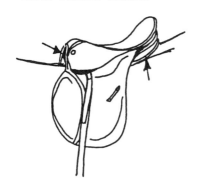

Around the gullet and under the edge of the seat the nails holding the panel in place often come loose. Check these occasionally as they can stick through and cause damage. Nails under the throat can injure the horse and loosen the front end of the saddle. Check these everytime you saddle, if they are loose get your saddlemaker to refit them.

- TILT BACK HEADS - Provide a lower profile.
- CONTACT SADDLES - Have smaller, thinner panels.
- FORWARD OR BACK SLANT FLAPS - Depends on your use. The forward, shorter flaps are for jumping.
- CATALOG SADDLES - You can order and construct your own saddle with different styles and amenities.
- EUROPEAN SADDLES - Have the best leather quality. Soon will be available direct from the manufacturer.
- CHECK the 'twist' as many saddles have too much rafter.
- TRY SADDLES OUT BEFORE YOU BUY THEM.

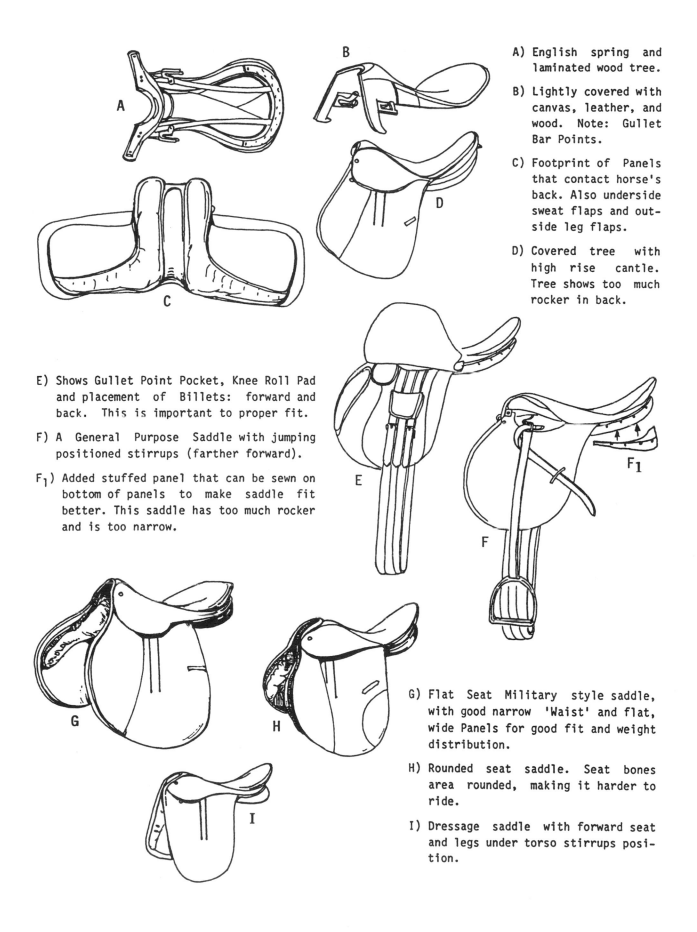

A) English spring and laminated wood tree.

B) Lightly covered with canvas, leather, and wood. Note: Gullet Bar Points.

C) Footprint of Panels that contact horse's back. Also underside sweat flaps and outside leg flaps.

D) Covered tree with high rise cantle. Tree shows too much rocker in back.

E) Shows Gullet Point Pocket, Knee Roll Pad and placement of Billets: forward and back. This is important to proper fit.

F) A General Purpose Saddle with jumping positioned stirrups (farther forward).

F₁) Added stuffed panel that can be sewn on bottom of panels to make saddle fit better. This saddle has too much rocker and is too narrow.

G) Flat Seat Military style saddle, with good narrow 'Waist' and flat, wide Panels for good fit and weight distribution.

H) Rounded seat saddle. Seat bones area rounded, making it harder to ride.

I) Dressage saddle with forward seat and legs under torso stirrups position.

THE CORRECT SADDLE AND LOW NECK LINE
ARE NEEDED FOR COLLECTION

**WEIGHT AND
COLLECTION**

We have weighed some horses and found that approximately 55% of the weight of the horse is carried by the front legs and 45% by the back legs when the horse has its head and neck in the normal position. If the head and neck are raised - as much as 80 pounds or more (depending on the size of the horse) is transferred to the back end. If a 125 pound rider is added, they may displace a split in the weight of 80 pounds back and 45 pounds forward - when in the center of the saddle.

If the rider is in the 'chair seat', an additional 20 to 30 pounds with this size of rider maybe added to the original 80 to 100 pounds mentioned above and transferred to the back end of the horse. The net result of these figures; 80 + 20 pounds or more is now carried by the hinds, if the neck is high and the rider is sitting back. Add the 80 pound shift of the horse's weight, or (80 + 80 + 20) 180 pounds.

Even a casual observer can easily see the difference in the horse's action when over weighted on the back end. The stride by the hinds is greatly shortened and does not come up under your 'pockets' as with a forward position rider and a natural level head and neck. This obviously caves in the back and destroys good collection.

When testing further - the horse with a raised head and neck line - dropped its back as much as 4 inches below the back of the saddle. When the head and neck were lowered to a normal position or lower the back rounded up and came up to the saddle.

Use your seat and the reins to make the horse go natural.

The bareback seat

A 'caved' in back is much weaker - whoever sees a horse climb a hill with a high head - and the essence of good balanced collection is when the hinds come well forward and balances the weight of the horse.

The conclusion to these facts is: that a good collected horse is ridden with a saddle that places the rider in the center of the saddle and one rides the horse with a low neck line. The face maybe a little 'flat', but the neck is in or near the natural position for collection.

YOU CAN'T ACHIEVE GOOD COLLECTIONS
WITHOUT THE PROPER SADDLE.

THE RIDER'S WAIST AND WEIGHT

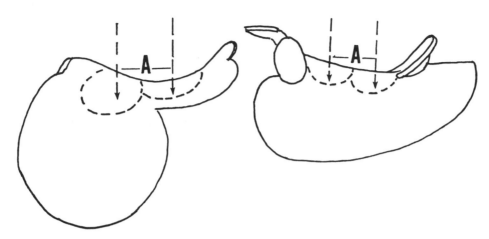

WHERE THE WEIGHT GOES

Distance (A) represents the distance from the crotch bones to the stirrup leathers - a distance of normally 5 or 6 inches.

Distance (A) represents the rider's weight (the torso and the legs). Distance (A) varies with the size of the rider. But (A) should be placed as near the middle of the saddle as possible - front to back. This is so the rider's weight is then evenly spread over the entire surface of the bars. This includes part of the pocket and part of the crown.

THE RIDER'S WEIGHT IS IN THE MIDDLE OF A GOOD SADDLE

The forward line of the seat pocket is the stirrup line. Generally, 5" or 6" ahead of the low spot of the seat.

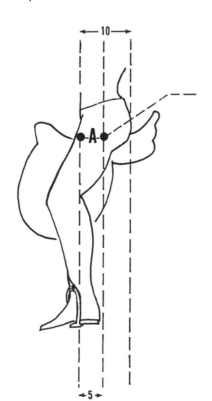

Rider takes up about 10"

The low spot of the seat

Distance (A) is in the middle of the saddle bars.

CHECK LIST FOR SELECTING A SADDLE

. PROPER FIT ON THE HORSE
   1) FITS WITHERS   3) FITS UNDER CANTLE
   2) FITS INTO SWALE (NO BRIDGING)   4) DOES NOT FIT OVER LAST RIB

. SADDLE POCKET IS IN MIDDLE OF THE SADDLE BARS

. PROPER SELECTION OF FORKS, SWELLS OR POMMEL OVER WITHERS

. STIRRUP LINE 5 to 6 INCHES AHEAD OF CENTER SEAT POCKET

. PROPER SELECTION OF RIGGING (GIRTHS, CINCHES, AND RIGGING) SO IT FITS THE
  THE HORSE'S BACK CORRECTLY

. SEAT FLAT UNDER SEAT BONES AND CROWN IS NARROW AHEAD OF THE CROTCH

. SKIRTS ALL ONE PIECE

. GOOD SKIRT LINER THAT WILL NOT CRAWL AND STRINGS ARE UNDER LINER

. BARS ARE CONCAVE OR FLAT UNDER CANTLE

. 4 to 6 INCHES OF BARS BEHIND CANTLE

. CORRECT CANTLE SELECTION - PROPER HORN AND SWELLS SELECTION

. FITS NARROW BETWEEN YOUR LEGS

. FREE SWINGING STIRRUPS

. GOOD TUNNEL DOWN UNDERSIDE OF SADDLE, ESPECIALLY ENGLISH SADDLES

. PANELS NOT TOO CLOSE TOGETHER TO FREE UP BACKBONE ON MANY ENGLISH SADDLES

. QUALITY LEATHER IS IMPORTANT FOR LONG LIFE OF SADDLE

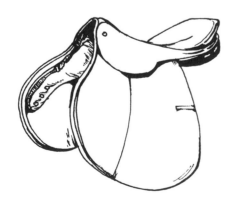

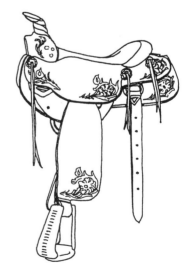

CARE OF THE SADDLE

Suggestions for long term care of your saddle:

1) Place the saddle on a saddle rack after use - so the leathers, fenders, and skirts do not dry bent and out of place after use. This can make the saddle uncomfortable to ride and start the leather to cracking. If the saddle is going to be there for a long time 'stick the stirrups' so they do not turn sideways.

2) Make sure you do not put the wet saddle pads or blankets under or on top of the saddle - preventing it from drying after use.

3) In cold weather, do not leave the saddle out in the barn or trailer because it cannot dry out and mold will start to grow in the leather. This will damage the leather. Move the saddles and bridles, etc. indoors to a dry place. If you have to leave them outdoors, cover them with a blanket or horse blanket, etc., and make sure they are completely covered. Do not use plastic.

If you are using your saddle everyday, like a trainer, and it is damp and cold, be sure to dry it out each night. Once the leather gets damp - like around the spot where the stirrups hang in the stirrup leathers - it can tear very easily under stress. Also, the cantle binding, horn covers, or the stitching will rot out. Dry them out each night!

If you are riding in very sloppy conditions - oil or soap your saddle at least once a week after it has dried out.

IMPORTANT FEATURE Leather that gets wet or damp does not last and gets stiff and cracks or tears under stress.

4) I like to keep a can of soft tallow near the hitching rail and, after my last horse for the day, I wipe the saddle down with a sponge or paint brush. I make sure the wear spots are coated liberally. The more you use the saddle, the more you have to care for it.

Sweat is harmful to leather

Dry climates are just as hard on leather as are damp climates.

CARING, CLEANING AND OILING

1) Wash the saddle down with a light soap (Murphy Oil Soap works well). Clean the soap off well. Do not let it dry too fast - like in the hot sun - put it in the shade.

2) Coat it out with a good light oil - just a very light coat is all that is necessary. Too heavy a coat changes the color too dark and gets on your clothing when you ride. Let it soak in for at least an hour. Oiling is only needed once or twice a year.

3) Next, with a good tallow, like a saddle soap or lanolin base saddle dressing, give the saddle a thorough coating. Especially over the wear spots. Let it set for a couple of hours to dry well, then rub it out with a dry cloth.

4) If a shiny finish is wanted, there are several products on the market or use shoe polish. A shiny finish makes the saddle slick and harder to ride.

CARING FOR THE LEATHER MAKES A SADDLE HOLD ITS VALUE AND PROVIDE MUCH LONGER SERVICE.

RUB IT IN GOOD

MY EXPERIENCE WITH SADDLES

I was introduced to the proper saddle for the proper fit on a horse while working for a large riding stable. At times, we saddled 10 to 30 head of horses per hour and had a remuda of 100 to 150 horses. The bunkhouse and equipment shed had over 100 saddles to select from. You did not have time to be very 'picky', you just had to make the best choice you could. If you 'sored up'a horse's back you were in 'deep' trouble.

In addition, I worked on other ranches and dude outfits where we were saddling many different horses all day.

With my own training operation, I have always used a large selection of saddles to fit the varying styles of backs we were confronted with each day. Some days we would work 5 or 6 head, other days 14 to 15 head, each horse had its own requirements for a saddle fit. Out of this I have developed a strong 'curiosity' about saddles. You have to try a large number of them before you realize there is a vast difference in saddles.

I have made saddles and have remodeled saddles and have a fairly complete leather shop on my ranch.

Out of this, the trees are the most important aspect of a saddle. The leather is like upholstery, it does not make the saddle - the tree does.

THINK OF THE HORSES AND GET SADDLES THAT FIT

87

NO ONE TALKS ABOUT SADDLE FIT IN TODAY'S MARKET

The saddle market today is not geared to saddle fit. Poor fit is common - good fit is uncommon. If you value your horse's comfort, you should not accept anything less. Manufacturers believe the horse market does not know any better or care and does not ride enough to make any difference. Saddle fitting is not easy - but it is worth the effort. There are saddle and tree manufacturers that are trying very hard to supply trees that fit. I have given you some basics for fitting - you will have to do the searching, fitting, and trying.

NO ONE TALKS ABOUT CARVING A GROUND SEAT JUST FOR YOU.

Getting the saddle to be comfortable for you is tied to finding a saddlemaker that is good at carving the ground seat and is willing to work with you. It will take 4 or 5 sittings and it will take acute observations and directions. It is not easy, but you can talk, unlike the horse. Using examples of saddles that you like the seat in, is especially helpful to the saddlemaker.

Sellers wish saddle fit for the horse and rider would go away, but you should make it the primary issue of the sale.

FINDING THE CORRECT TREE

You can work with your local saddlemaker to select from his tree selections, which is the quickest, or call some of the tree manufacturers. Some sell direct, others do not. Place the tree on the horse to measure the fit before you buy.

BUILDING A GROUND SEAT

Building a GOOD ground seat depends on the skill of the saddlemaker. Do some research here before you make a choice.

THE SEAT

The seat of the saddle should be over the low spot on the horse's back, generally just behind the withers, or often referred to as the bareback-seat-location. The back half of the seat is best nearly flat and the front half is very narrow. The seat bones sit on the back half and the crotch sits on the front half. The shaping or carving of this seat shape and its location forward over the low spot on the horse's back or farther back in the 'chair seat' location are the function of the saddlemaker.

PICK A GOOD SADDLEMAKER. HE WILL GET THE JOB DONE RIGHT.

LOOKING FOR THE RIGHT SADDLE

ROCKER. The bars should bow out underneath to fit the hollow behind the withers. Most saddles bridge from the withers to the middle of the back.

Many English saddles do not fit the back well; too narrow up front and not wide and flat enough under the seat.

Many Western saddles are too long, plus the rider's weight is not in the middle of the saddle; because the stirrups are too far forward and the seat is too far back.

GOOD EXAMPLES:
Visalia
Louellen
Ropers
Association

The treemakers are the problem. Saddlemakers are generally just upholsterers or coverers.

The 3 things to look for in getting the proper saddle for performance riding are: (1) the plate, the top of the saddle seat between the pommel and cantle, is flat or nearly flat so the rider can move forward and back, (2) the stirrups are not too far forward, so one cannot get their feet under themselves and achieve a stand-up seat without pressing back into the cantle, and (3) the rigging, or billets, and the tree will allow the saddle to be placed far enough forward so the rider is close to the bareback position and not too far back on the horse's back.

This is not a dressage seat, but somewhere between a deep seat position and a dressage seat. If you read the various publications you can see the winners of Western Equitation generally riding this seat, or photos of the U.S. Cavalry, or old cowboys, or the American Indians. Many top reining and horse trainers use this seat. It really works. Most eventing riders and the best of polo players achieve this kind of seat at speed.

Without a good 'lock' on the horse to hold yourself on in the rough spots, and forward and balanced over the horse, you can't expect the optimum performance out of the horse. In addition, without a good seat you won't have a good set of sensitive hands. NO SEAT - NO HANDS! Most factory made saddles are made for beginners and are deep seat equitation saddles, where one rides on the cantle and too far back with the feet forward...your feet and legs push you back into the cantle. The professional cowboy saddles, rancher saddles, old time U.S. Cavalry officer saddles, or English eventing saddles are better examples.

Getting the position right first is 75% of the task and that is mostly saddle. You have to have the correct _profile_ to begin with before you ride.

Today, there are more good English flat saddles for performance than Western stock saddles. Before the 50's there were more good Western saddles available. We can thank manufacturers for this. Good teachers and trainers know good saddles, but manufacturers are more interested in building beginner or equitation saddles than stand-up seat saddles. The trouble lies in the tree (frame) and the younger saddlemakers, who have no experience with stand-up seat saddles. Once you can spot a stand-up seat saddle and understand the equation of throat, stirrups, plate and rigging, you will start to see them. Saddlemakers that make working stock saddles for working cowboys and ranchers are a good source.

ROCKER EFFECT

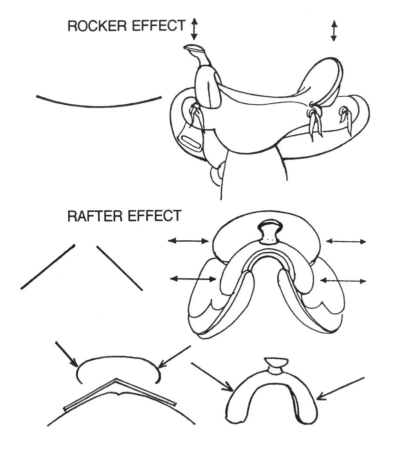

Rock the saddle up and down at these points and see if it rocks up and down on either end.

This indicates if the 'BOW' (or bottom curve) of the saddle bars marry up to the horse's back; it sits flat without any rocking.

Too much 'rocker' or too little - both sore a horse's back.

RAFTER EFFECT

Press here, on both sides of the cantle, and see if the saddle fits down on the horse's back. Look at it from the back. See if the angles of the back match those of the saddle.

Now press down on the forks, or the pommel, and see if the saddle rides up on the back, or belly flops down on the backbone. Either way is bad. Now rock it side to side to see if it is fitting securely. Get around and look under the front of the saddle.

SITTING FLAT ON THE BACK

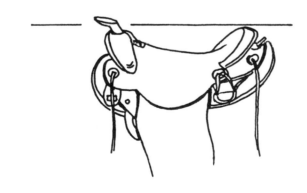

This is very important - or it pushes you to the back of the saddle. The saddle should fit flat.

Do not put large thick pads under the front of the saddle that will cause the front to climb-up over the withers and tilt back. Get a wider saddle or thinner blankets. Thick pads are bad for this. Besides, this burns the top of the withers, rubbing back and forth.

MAKE SURE THE BLANKETS FIT

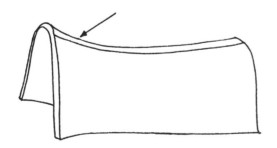

Make sure the sweat blankets, if you use them, fit flat and do not wrinkle after you put the pad on next. Many saddle blankets, if the weave is not correct, wrinkle just behind the withers when the pad or the saddle go on and this sores up the back. Some pads are also this way. Examine this carefully. The higher the withers, the more this happens.

SADDLES FOR PERFORMANCE RIDING

SADDLES
Getting off the cantle and in the middle of the saddle.

Deep Seat Saddles are very comfortable, but only good for short pleasure riding.

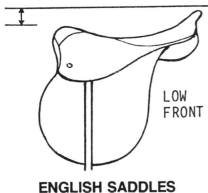

LOW FRONT

ENGLISH SADDLES

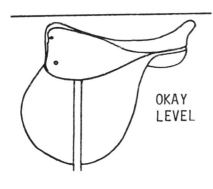

OKAY LEVEL

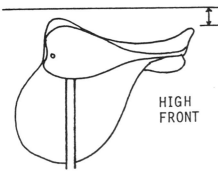

HIGH FRONT

The seat is largely dictated by the saddle and a little practice by the rider. Today, Western saddles are largely built to make riding easier, for the beginner, with a deep seat, or 'chair seat', (the rider looks like he/she is sitting in a chair - rather than standing on the horse). Our grandfathers would not have liked most of our modern saddles because of the 'deep seat' and 7/8" rigging that keeps the saddle too far back. Also, the plate, or top of the saddle, needs to be flat from front to back so the rider can move forward or back as needed. Moving gives the rider the ability to signal the horse; forward to free up the hinds for lead changes, etc., and back for anchoring the hinds for spins, turn arounds, front end lead changes, etc. Modern equitation saddles, or Western deep seat saddles, are comfortable at slow speeds, but not good for fast performance or long distance riding.

If the west had been settled with these saddles, the horses' backs would have been so sore the migration would have ended at the Mississippi.

English saddles have a common fault, too, in that most are built as an all purpose saddle - half for jumping and half for performance. Most are too deep seated. Yet, there are forward seat saddles and there are deep seat jumping saddles. The jumping saddles are too deep seated - made to free up the front end of the horse to clear the jumps. The forward dressage saddles have the stirrups too far back for performance riding. The average English saddle is built to try to suit everyone, but it doesn't work. Eventing saddles come the closest to being a good performance saddle. Many English saddles tip back, or downhill, too often. Look for the low point in the seat to be no more than 4" behind the stirrup hangers and the girth billets near 3" behind the stirrup hangers. (This may vary with the style of tree).

Large flat and wide pads under the seat are important so as not to make the back sore. Once sore, the horse does not work correctly. Many newer models have only metal tubes for the tree bars and these 'point load' right through, no matter what type of padding is used under them. The flat bars are still the best. Too narrow in the pommel is another common fault and this sores the top of the scapula and makes the saddle sit too high in front. The saddle should sit level.

WESTERN SADDLES

4 to 5 "

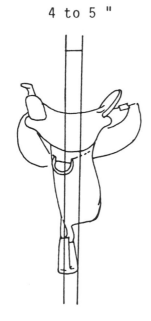

The plate should be fairly flat, not tipped uphill to the forks (front). The main thing to observe is the relationship between the low point in the saddle plate, the stirrups, and the cinch 'D' rings. The low point should not be more than 4 or 5 inches behind the stirrups and the cinch 'D' rings should be only 2 or 3 inches ahead of the stirrups. (This may vary depending on the type of back the saddle is built to fit.) The low point on the plate and the stirrups is the critical point.

The tree must allow the saddle to be placed well 'forward' up on the back side of the withers, and yet not override the back of the scapula bones, and yet be level on the top plate. If the cinch 'D's are too far forward, the saddle will always ride back too far. Examine this carefully, or the saddle will always crawl back and cause the back to be sore near the withers. For most horses, 5/8 to 3/4 rigging is a better fit. For full flat backed Quarter Horses, or work horses used as saddle horses, the full double is best. The best way to test this is to lay your arm on the scapula bone and the fingers should point right at the horn of the saddle if it is in the correct position. The throat of the forks, or pommel, is also very critical, that it fits comfortably when in the right position.

If the stirrup leathers are well forward, then the plate must be flat so the rider can get forward and over the stirrups when the horse is moving fast. If the stirrups are back a little farther, say an inch or so, the rider does not have to move forward so far to get off the seat of his pants and over the stirrups...and out of the chair.

Riding in the middle of the saddle (bars) is good for the horse because it proportions out the weight over the bars. It is also the best position for good equitation.

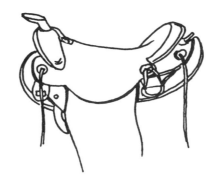

WESTERN SADDLES

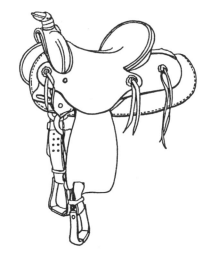

The same formula mentioned before for English saddles is almost the same for Western saddles. The low point of the seat should not be more than 4" or 5" behind the stirrups and the top plate should be fairly flat. The cinch "D's" should not be but 2" or 3" ahead of the stirrup leathers. The cantle may or may not be forward near the low point in the plate. Some are and some are not. On some roping saddles they sit farther back. The 'old timer' saddles were this way and on the bronc saddles the cantle was farther forward. The critical measurement is, does the saddle sit forward up to the scapula bones and the 'D' rings are so placed to help hold it in place. Plus, the relationship between the low point of the seat and the stirrup leathers. The throat (fork) of these saddles has to fit the withers as well as the slope of the back under the seat, sloping at the same angle. Too high or too flat causes sore backs. In addition, the bars should fit down into the 'swale', or concave indentation, behind the withers or the saddle will bridge between the withers and the deep back of the horse causing a bad sore under the seat. The crown of the plate should not be too wide, narrower crowns are better suited for most riders. If the plate is flat, the stirrups can be a little farther forward as long as the rider can move forward and get 'over' the stirrups when the horse is moving fast.

The main things to look for are:

1. Low point in the middle of the saddle. "The seat".
2. Stirrups hanging only 4" to 5" ahead of low point.
3. A fairly flat plate. Not tilted up too high.
4. The plate has a narrow crown.
5. The stirrups are free swinging; forward and back.
6. Preferably rigged at 3/4 to 5/8 depending on the horse.
7. Pommel or fork sits well on the 'back' of withers.
8. Good bars that slope correctly for the horse, scapula to last rib.
9. Good deep curve to bars to fit into 'dip' behind the withers.
10. 5" or 6" of bar behind cantle.
11. Thick skirting leather to spread weight of rider.
12. The bars are well rounded up on the edges, especially in the front and the rear. Thin or sharp bars on the tree cause sore backs.
13. The low point of the seat is over the low point of the back. Basically, a performance saddle should put you within a few inches of the spot you would be if you were riding bareback. Most saddles move you behind this position.

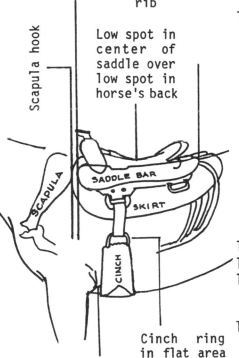

Bar 2" back

Bars do not go over last rib

Scapula hook

Low spot in center of saddle over low spot in horse's back

Cinch ring in flat area

Cinch does not go over webbing

93

The saddle puts you on the sweet spot, or neutral zone (usually the low spot).

You can reach the <u>neutral spot</u> or <u>sweet spot</u> on the horse's back easier this way. (You can feel it when you are there). There are no G's pulling on you, or pushing on you, it is sort of a neutral zone. Once you find it - I guarantee you will keep looking for it - because it is the easiest place to ride. Stand up, then sit down, straight down over the horse, and you will find it. Just keep doing it. You see a lot of fellows pull themselves forward with the saddle horn to find his position - when the saddle is too deep-seated. Stand up, ride a ways, then sit down slowly and - make it straight down - this will put you on the sweet spot.

Many of the Western saddles built before World War II were built correctly.
There are many around built later, but you have to look for them. Most ranch saddles are this way. Most Association trees are good this way or variations.

Many military flat saddles are good, or forward seat saddles with flat seats.

Too wide, or narrow.

Many flat backed saddles do not have enough bowing out on the bars (the underside of the tree) (like the bottom of a ship's hull) to drop into the curve of the back just behind the withers, and wind up causing the saddle to bridge from the withers to the middle of the back. This causes a real sore spot, in time, on the horse's back and affects his performance, and yours too.

A short backed horse with some withers and a long sloping shoulder needs a saddle that curves into the back this way.

It is easy to look at a saddle and see if the plate is flat and the rigging (where the cinch, or girth, attaches to the tree) is set (say) at 3/4 or 5/8ths. But it is hard to see if the tree is built properly to sit far enough forward on the horse to put the rider in the bareback position. It is also hard to see if the cantle is far enough forward and the stirrups are hung properly for performance riding.

The easiest way is to get into the saddle - put your weight into the stirrups and see if you can hold a stand up position without being forced back to the cantle.

One quick way to look for proper placement of the saddle on the back, is to lay your arm up along the scapula, or shoulder blade, and your hand should touch the fork, or pommel, of the saddle. Be careful the saddle does not get down on the withers, that can make it very sore, or that the tree is too narrow and pinches the withers, that is also very bad.

Another aspect of good riding requires that the stirrups be free swinging, so they will swing forward and back in a full arc. Not locked in the straight up and down position. Athletic performance riding requires the stirrups to move, so you can keep your feet under yourself at all times.

The peak of the saddle is important. That is, is the plate very broad, or comes to a peak? Depending on your build, too wide a plate will hurt your riding. Narrow peaks, or crowns, are better for most of us.

94

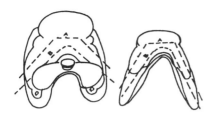

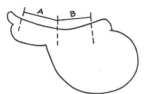

Helps if seat
bones area is
flat yet crown
is rounded-up.

STIRRUPS

Put a stick through
your stirrups when
you put them up.

Bars behind
the cantle

It takes more time to put a crown in a saddle, so this is usually left out. But this will give you a better chance to get your legs straighter down under your weight and this also gives you more 'grip' on the horse. You stay on better.

Avoid thick English knee rolls that extend back under your legs. These widen your grip and cut down on your 'clinch', or 'grip', on the sides of the horse. Thick Western stirrup leathers and stirrup fenders, as they come over the skirting under your thighs, can make the saddle too wide for a good seat. Old time saddles were especially good in this area of construction with thinner quality leather used for stirrup leathers and fenders. The skirting leather on Western saddles should be thick, but not as skirting leather.

Platform stirrups seem to be more common where one can ride on the balls of their feet to give a little more cushion in controlling their up and down weight and getting off the seat of their pants and certain riding cues. Two inches or so seems workable. They should also be twisted back so they hang correctly when a horseback, not rotating back trying to turn flat sideways, putting stress on your ankles. This is more than one can keep track of and ride well, too.

If you ride green or 'broncy' horses, then opt for the narrower ones and put your foot deep in the stirrup. A good Association saddle makes a good choice for a colt saddle. It will give a good seat for colts and a fair performance seat besides. Be sure the stirrup leathers will kick forward easily and not hang up on the stirrup-cut-out or anything when a horseback. Many old time high backs with good swells are good for this type of work.

On Western saddles make sure the bars extend out behind the cantle a good 5" or 6", not including the leather jockey or skirting. If they are too short, they will sore a horse's back up for sure on long or hard rides. This causes the horse to shorten his stride behind and go kind of peg legged in back. They should go up to the last rib only.

BREAST COLLAR

Your saddle-maker has to buy the tree and may have to look a-round some to find the correct tree for your horse.

Many saddles need a breast collar to keep them forward. It is the rare saddle that does not need a breast collar to keep it in the correct position. I like to hook the collar off the saddle D's with a neck keeper, or strap over the neck, to keep the collar from getting too low. Too high cuts off the horse's wind.

The very best way to see if the saddle will fit the horse is to place just the tree on the back and make a judgment. One method used for years is to dust the bottom of the saddle with flour then put it on the bare back of the horse. Do not move it, but just lift it directly straight up and off and see if the back is evenly covered with flour dust. One saddle will not fit all horses, and, if you ride many different horses, you will probably have several saddles to fit the different backs. The first thing in ordering a saddle is to have the saddle fitted to the horse's back first, then the rider. In this case, the tree has to be shaped and fitted to the horse first before anything takes place. All bars are generally the same, made out of 2x6's. You may have to do some shopping here.

The first thing about a saddle is, does it fit your horse? Second thing is, does it fit you?

GENERAL SADDLE COMMENTS

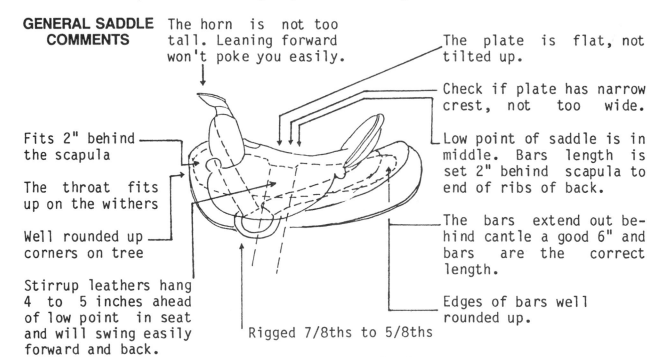

The horn is not too tall. Leaning forward won't poke you easily.

The plate is flat, not tilted up.

Check if plate has narrow crest, not too wide.

Fits 2" behind the scapula

The throat fits up on the withers

Well rounded up corners on tree

Stirrup leathers hang 4 to 5 inches ahead of low point in seat and will swing easily forward and back.

Low point of saddle is in middle. Bars length is set 2" behind scapula to end of ribs of back.

The bars extend out behind cantle a good 6" and bars are the correct length.

Edges of bars well rounded up.

Rigged 7/8ths to 5/8ths

Check the slope of the bars match the slope of the horse's back, both in front and over the back. RAFTER EFFECT.

Good convex form the long ways so bars will drop into hollow behind the withers. Otherwise, the saddle bridges from the withers to the small of the back. ROCKER EFFECT

96

RIGGING AND CINCHES
BILLETS AND GIRTHS

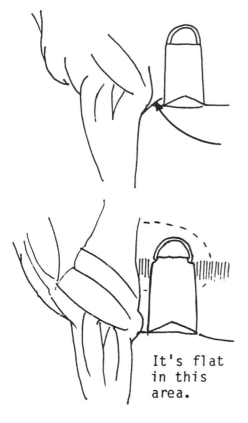

It's flat in this area.

Most western saddles today are rigged at three-quarter to full double because of the influence and demand for many low withered show type Quarter Horses. The more withers the horse has, the more likely it will have a slope to the shoulder and the need to have the rigging in a range of three-quarter to five-eighths. Performance horses, or sport horses, are more inclined to have more withers and more slope to the shoulder. With the girth or rigging "D's" back farther, it keeps the saddle forward on the withers and keeps the saddle from slipping back. In addition, it keeps the cinch, or girth, off the webbing behind the leg.

This placement is also important for English saddles as well. If the billets are too far forward, the saddle tends to ride back on withered horses. The farther back, the more the saddle tends to stay forward. The wider the upper shoulders, as in the difference in horses today, will also cause it to slide back. Examine this point.

The cinches/girths should comfortably fit behind the webbing of the horse's forearm and before the barrel gets too wide.

Do not go over the webbing

The ends of the cinches/girths should end just above the widest part of the barrel.

A wider cinch/girth is better than a narrow one because it spreads the pressure out and is harder to make the saddle slip sideways. The cinch rings won't make the barrel sore if they are above the turning edge of the barrel. Cinches too short tend to make the rings dig into the barrel where it turns under. Keep the rings, latigos, half breeds, straight up and down as much as you can, not turning under.

Saddles with multiple rigging locations are available and very handy when using the saddle on many different horses. On old U.S. Cavalry saddles, the rigging D's could be adjusted forward or back, by adjusting the back rigging strap.

The better fit a saddle has the less you have to cinch up. Don't ever bet a cowboy that he can take the cinch off and still get on unless you are the first one to try. On a good fitting saddle, if you don't break the suction, you usually can get on <u>one</u> time without the cinch. The second time, if the cowboy breaks the suction getting off, you won't get on a second time, no matter how close you keep to the horse.

ENGLISH SADDLES Narrower saddles are for smaller riders and wider saddles are for larger riders. The saddles that tip up hill too much keep you back in the chair seat - make sure the saddle will be nearly flat on the horse. If the throat of the pommel is too high and too narrow, it will tip the saddle back and pinch the withers on each side. Make sure the saddle fits with about 2 inches above the withers. In addition, as mentioned before, take caution that the bars of the saddle are not metal tubing that will effect point loading and sore the horse's back. Be sure the pads under the seat are large enough to carry the weight. They should be a good 6 inches wide or more on each side.

Sore backed horses do not perform well and only get worse rather than better.

POINTS TO
LOOK FOR

Saddle fits
nearly level

Stirrup hangers
3 or 4 inches
ahead of low
point in saddle
seat.

Billet position
depends on the
horse. Prefer-
ably under the
low point in
seat or the
stirrup hangers

Low point of
saddle lines up
with low point
on horse's back
just behind the
withers.

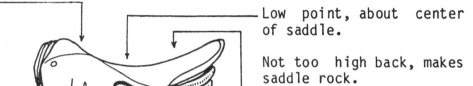
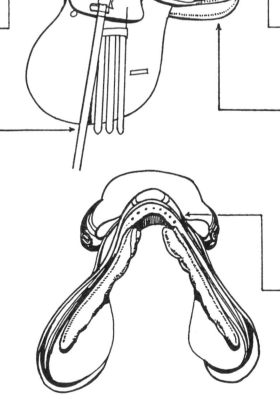

Low point, about center
of saddle.

Not too high back, makes
saddle rock.

Near flat, not rounded.

Flexible throat, not
rigid. Not too narrow.

Wide enough in back to
carry weight.
Good cushion quality.

Tree bars are wide enough
and do not ride over the
scapula.

Make sure the saddle fits
the back.

Open throat, not too
narrow or too wide, fits
2 inches or so above the
withers.

Bars should have some
flexibility on throat,
not stiff, but 'springy'.

Saddle is correct length
(from scapula hook to
last rib).

THE GROUND SEAT The ground seat is what makes the difference; where the low point in the seat is located.

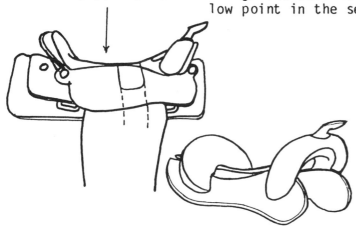

Also, the stirrup leather cut-outs locate the stirrups.
(1) How far they swing, and (2) How far forward or back on the saddle.

The bars are generally all the same, except for length which is bad. The fork and the cantle are then added for whatever style has been ordered. This then varies the placement of the bars; the width, pitch (rafter), but not the rocker.

The seat, stirrups, and rigging can be changed. The seat may be one or two layers thick over a sheet metal underseat.

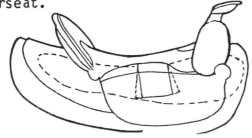

When the leather is added, it's the foundation seat, or ground seat, that locates the low point in the saddle.

The same is true for the placement of the stirrups, forward and back. It is done about this same time and can vary depending on where the cut-out is placed.

Saddles are made for the largest part of the market - so whatever is most popular gets built whether it is best, good, or right does not make any difference. What is good for the horse and rider does not count.

If the crown is too wide or flat it will be harder to ride. A narrower crown with flat pocket is best for the average sized person. It costs more to have a good crown and pocket. They are usually too wide on the run of the mill saddles.

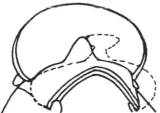

Check the skirt strings that they do not go over the sheepskin; should be recessed into the sheepskin.

THE GROUND SEAT may tip up too far forward, keeping you in the pocket, but limiting your move forward or back for signaling with the seat position. If the high front of the seat holds you back behind the center of the saddle this is the wrong saddle for the stand-up seat. (NOTE:) Some bronc saddles are higher in front to help the rider from the downward thrust and gives better grip.

Feel the bottom of the skirts for any ridges caused by the 'plugs' or overlapping of leather on the top layer of the skirt. This skirt is not all one piece, but is usually made of several makeshift pieces or scraps. If the pieces are overlapped, you have a ridge you can feel if you run your hands hard over the underside of the skirting. The skirting should go all the way and be 5/16 to 7/16 thick. To spread the weight get stiff skirts.

ENGLISH RIGGING

Most English saddles give you 3 billets for girth adjustment which is not quite enough with today's variety of horses. Girth placement helps locate the saddle forward, to a large degree. Many English saddles tend to slide back down off the withers and need the back billets to help hold it in place, along with a breast collar and a leveling pad of some sort under the back of the saddle.

GET IT LEVEL

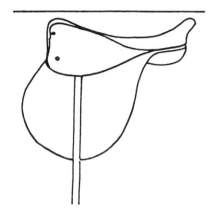

The leveling pad is very important in getting the saddle into a level profile, otherwise it is apt to tip backwards throwing the rider out of the seat and to the back of the saddle.

Missing the webbing in back of the horse's legs is also important in the placement of the girth. Make sure the horse's legs are not angled backwards when taking up the girth.

I like the Argentine saddles with the leather cinch (like a Western saddle) better than the buckles and billets. It gets the saddle down on the horse much better and firmer, because the rigging straps pull the front and the back of the saddle down, not just the middle.

THE CORRECT THROAT

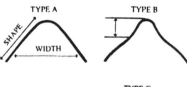

The narrow throat of the English saddle necessitates that you use a fairly light pad, otherwise the pad will force the throat of the saddle up in the air above the withers. If the throat is too narrow, it will ride high and back too far, if too wide it slopes down over the withers and may ride on the withers themselves, possibly causing a sore. This sore could easily lead to a fistula (infection in this area which is extremely difficult to cure). So, the correct throat in an English saddle is very important in the selection. Try it before you buy it.

FLAT CROWNS

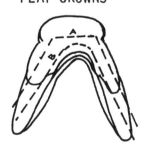

KNEE ROLLS

I like flat seats rather than ones that have some roll to them, for staying on in rough riding situations. If the seat crown is rounded all the way to the back of the saddle, you will find it harder to ride, than if the seat portion near the back of the saddle is somewhat flat.

Knee rolls are a matter of preference, however for many, if they are too thick or wide, they make the horse seem too wide between the knees. This makes your knees hurt after awhile. Pay attention that they do not make the saddle too wide in this area, but just on the outer edge of the panel.

PURCHASING SADDLES

Get a saddler that will try different trees on your horse and help you select the best fit. He can also make modifications by gluing layers of leather and shaping the bottom side of the bars to fit the back. Then get the saddle made to fit you; the crown, position of the stirrups, the rigging, and a flat plate with a low pocket in the near middle of the saddle.

BENEFITS TO STAND-UP SEAT

1) Stops bouncing.
2) Keeps knees from hurting.
3) Makes horse perform better.
4) Helps put weight in middle, or center of bars. Makes weight spread over horse's or mule's back evenly. Some mules won't go if weight is too far back. They stop.

STIRRUPS

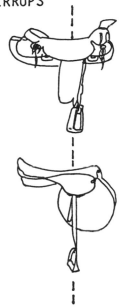

Stirrups and low point of saddle (pocket) should be nearly in the middle of the saddle. This puts weight of rider in the middle of the bars.

If the stirrups are too far forward the rider can't get off his pockets and the weight is concentrated on the back of the saddle and the deep back of the horse. This pushes the rider back, not up, out of balance and out of rhythm with the horse's movements.

Consequently, new post war saddlemakers make trees longer to compensate for the deep seat and spread the deep weight out over the back farther. But long bars cause bridging. The saddle bars should not be too long. They should end at the last ribs.

This sores up the back, raises the head, shortens the reach under hind stride, and cuts down on performance. The horse carries the weight best when the weight is in the middle of the saddle (length).

STAND-UP SADDLES

Old Western saddles, rancher saddles, frontier saddles. Many Early American saddles used centered seats (with the seat's low spot just behind the stirrups and in the middle of the saddle).

MODERN POST WAR SADDLES

Deep seated or out of balance saddles make back seat riders. Built for pleasure riding or the recreational market.

LEGS

A longer leg rider can sit back a little farther. Shorter needs to be just back of the stirrup. The low point in the plate is just back of stirrups 4" to 5". The taller you are this distance increases by a couple inches.

LENGTH OF SADDLE BARS

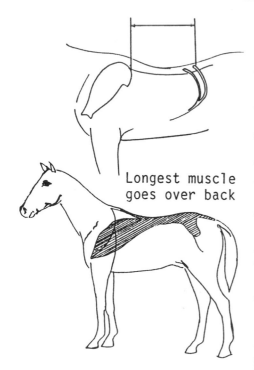

Longest muscle
goes over back

Most deep seat sad-
dles are too long
and go over the
last ribs.

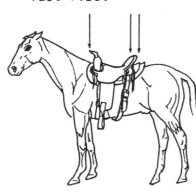

Hold your hand under
the back of saddle
then have someone
raise and lower the
horse's head. Feel
how the back raises
and lowers 2" to 3".

THE BACK BENDS UP AND
DOWN WHEN IN MOTION

I was always taught as a youngster, by old horsemen that had spent a lifetime using horses for traveling instead of cars, that you do not put the saddle back any farther than where the ribs end on the back bone; if you do you will sore up the back. These old timers were very <u>adamant</u> about this point.

The last rib connects into the backbone just ahead of the Thoracico Lumbar Joint. I looked it up! This is about 12" to 14" ahead of the Lumbosacral Joint (where the pelvis connects to the backbone). This Thoracico Lumbar Joint has a certain degree of flexibility - up and down. In addition, the longest muscle on the horse, the Longissimus Dorsi, and the Dorsal Ligament cross over each other at this point. Also, this is where the ends of the big Gluteus Medius muscle come over the pelvis and tie into the back. Also, just in back of the last rib are the wings of the vertebrae that stick out 5" or 6" on either side of the main column of the back-bone. The significance of this is: where the muscles have the ribs under them, they can carry weight, but just back a few inches there is the opening between the ribs and the vertebrae wings that offers very little support.

So, if the bars of the saddle tree go over this area it will tire the back or sore it up and hinder the horse from extending his gaits or movements to their full range. The lack of support and the up and down motion are both to blame.

I have seen this happen many times over, especially with short backed horses. Many of the clinics I have had I find horses who are 'cranking' their tails or are a little 'broncy' - and sure enough - the saddles are 'bridging' from this very spot. Once corrected with the proper fitting saddle or 'bar length' the horses go relaxed. Thus, the bars cannot be too long.

I have seen this with Forest Service Pack Strings where they instructed everyone to keep the packs ahead of this point. The packers said this was the weakest point on the back and to keep everything ahead of it.

In addition, the back flexes from this point from the action of the Longissimus Dorsi Muscle on top of the back and the stretching out of the big muscle along the bottom of the stomach (the Rectus Abdominus). Then on

102

the next part of the stride just the opposite happens. The top stretches out and the bottom muscle contracts. This happens with every stride, especially at the gallop, making the back bend up and down just behind the ribs. This motion creates a whipping action along the top line that augments the action of the muscle groups in the hip and back legs and the shoulders and front legs. The back 'bows', springing up and down, supplementing the motion of the front and back legs. The head and neck counter balance this motion and act sort of as a damper or counter weight.

LENGTH OF BARS

The saddle bars, not the skirting, but the bars on the tree, for the comfort of the horse in motion, should not extend over this point on the back. With all this motion up and down and, if the back end of the saddle is overloaded, it will sore up the back for sure!

Use your fingers to find the last rib on the back.

Horses may put up with this and you will never know that your saddle is hurting because horses are very stoic about pain. But the outcome is the horse does not perform as well and is enduring discomfort. Use them right or don't use them at all.

The tendency with saddles that are too long is to bridge between the deep back and the withers. Horses and mules working in hilly country, fast and hard riding or long hard all day rides, will sore up a back even faster.

Pack saddles are generally shorter than many saddles. The reason explained to me is they can carry the weight better. It is amusing that mules will often times just stop and not move if their packs are hurting their backs. Then you have to stop and look for the problem. Too short is not good either.

THE SCAPULA

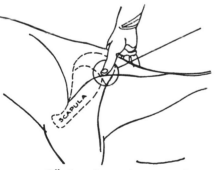

The scapula bone has a hook on the back side and at this point there are 4 muscles and/or ligaments connecting or passing over this spot. One of these is the Longissimus Dorsi. If you put your hand down over the back of the withers you can feel this 'knot' like spot on the back of the scapula. The front of the saddle bars should not rest on this area, but be about 2" behind it. The scapula is not attached to the backbone, but by ligaments, and moves with the action of the horse, plus the action of the muscles swelling and contracting and running across this area.

2" back gives the big muscles room to work over the top of the scapula.

The bars on the front of the saddle should be 4" or 5" wide and well rounded up on the edges, especially to avoid 'digging into' this area. The bars need to be a

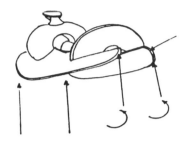

Be sure the bars have rounded-up ends both front and back.

good 2" thick to allow enough 'cupping or rounding-up effect' to settle into the hollow alongside the back of the withers. But, again, the saddle bars should not override this scapula hook.

Another critical aspect of the front of the saddle is how far down do the bars come over the sides of the horse and not ride forward over the top of the scapula cartlidge? (The top part that includes the hook).

The only way to establish this is to actually try the saddle on the horse without blankets and examine how it sits down over the withers. The back is sort of hollowed out and the bars will fall right into place if properly shaped. If the tree is too wide or narrow it will miss fitting into these areas. Make sure you allow for blankets and the tree is not too low.

CRITERIA FOR THE LENGTH OF THE BARS

Each horse has an exact length of bar that will fit his back properly. IT IS FROM 2" BEHIND THE SCAPULA HOOK, OR KNOT, TO THE LAST RIBS ON THE BACK.

USE YOUR ARM TO LOCATE SADDLE

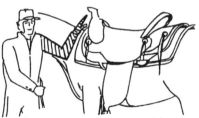

Lay your arm on the shoulder and point with the fingers. It should touch the horn or pommel.

A simple way to check your saddle position on the withers is to lay your forearm up the shoulder and your fingers should touch or point right to the top of the saddle horn, or pommel.

The top of the scapula is 3" or 4" below the top spine of the withers. The bottom moves more than the top, especially with athletic moves like jumping. The bars of the saddle need to be well padded and rounded up to accommodate the swelling and stretching of the muscles and the movement of the top of the scapula.

Horses accommodate for the saddle that hurts or is irritating and will shorten their stride or hesitate making athletic moves that you maybe asking. Even 1" too long is too long.

The saddle works best if we sit in the middle and the weight is evenly distributed over the bars.

The best place to ride is in the middle of the saddle and our weight is evenly distributed over the bars. If the weight is towards the back of the saddle, the back gets more weight than the front. The low point of the top plate should be near the middle to cause us to sit in this spot. Most riders are nearly 10" thick, so this will take up a good portion of the saddle seat. The stirrups help in distributing the weight also.

104

SORE SPOTS

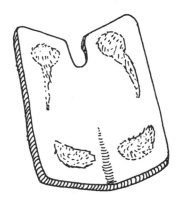

SHOWS CONTACT SPOTS

If you can find dry spots, or the hair looks matted, or the area is very slightly raised, your horse is having a sore back.

If the bars do not fit the back properly it either rafters or bridges and does not fit onto the back smoothly front to back. You will have a saddle that hurts the back. It does not make any difference how many pads you put on either, due to the principle of 'point loading' that transfers the load right through thick pads.

The best case scenario is to try out the tree on the horse's back before the leather is applied. The next best thing is to really investigate the fit by peering under the saddle.

BLANKETS

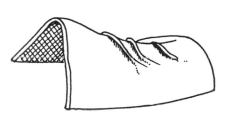

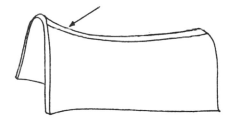

Blankets that are wool are still the best there is because they wick away the moisture and cool the back. Keeping the back cool is very important. It helps if air can get under the front of the saddle, like through the throat of the saddle under the forks.

Many pads that are combination materials wrinkle just in back of the withers and this is dangerous. Many materials walk with the motion and wrinkle and this is dangerous. Look out for these. Wool felt pads are good. Some materials walk on the horse's back with the motion and the hair is pulled out or cut off by the pad or blanket.

Sculptured pads or blankets, that are tailored to fit the back and go up on the withers, are excellent features. Some of the hospital pad materials used seem workable with these pads. The old style horse hair pads or wool felts are also good if you can find them.

BLANKETS/PADS UNDER THE FORKS OR THROAT

Adding too many pads under the forks or tunnel of the saddle over the withers just tightens the fit and raises the saddle up. This tight fit puts undue stress or pressure over the withers from the blankets or pads. This can cause a severe sore on the withers which, if infected, can cause a fistula. A fistula may take a year or so to cure or it may never cure.

Make sure you allow enough width in the selection of the forks or tunnel to fit the horse properly with the pads or blankets. Give this special attention.

105

English
performance
saddles have
free swing-
ing stirrup
leathers.

On some Western saddles the stirrups are too far forward and fixed in place so they won't swing freely. I have found by cutting the 'plugs' back 5/8-inch or so and at an angle, one can free the stirrups up and make them hang back a bit farther. This also gives one a freer swinging stirrup that stays under the rider when moving around in different athletic positions in the saddle. If the stirrups do not stay under the rider's weight - the rider loses his seat and rhythm on the horse. It is essential that one can get the stirrups well under their weight for a good stand-up seat.

UNPLUGGING THE SADDLE

1) Pull the top plate cover back, as pictured.

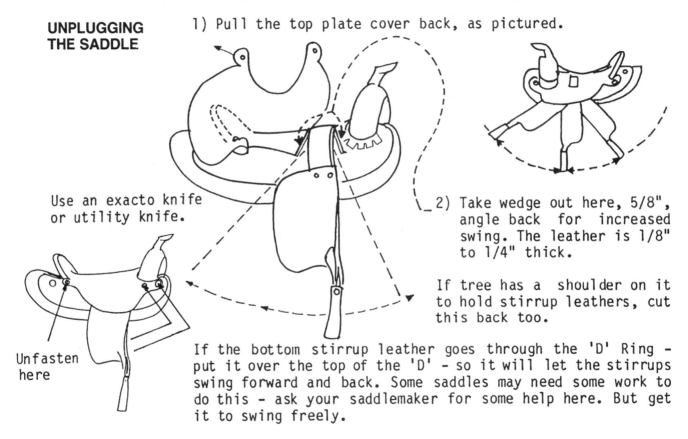

Use an exacto knife
or utility knife.

2) Take wedge out here, 5/8", angle back for increased swing. The leather is 1/8" to 1/4" thick.

If tree has a shoulder on it to hold stirrup leathers, cut this back too.

Unfasten
here

If the bottom stirrup leather goes through the 'D' Ring - put it over the top of the 'D' - so it will let the stirrups swing forward and back. Some saddles may need some work to do this - ask your saddlemaker for some help here. But get it to swing freely.

WHY DO THIS?

One way to fall or get bucked off a horse for sure is to have one rear, buck, stumble, or have the back end slip on the ice with stirrups that do not swing free. The rider loses his seat if the stirrups won't move with your lower leg. It is just as important that the stirrups go forward as back for the horse that is practicing standing on its head or on his hinds, or both, one after the other. If a horse bucks or jumps down something, his back may approach straight up and down - so you need stirrups to go forward. This way you can get your feet under you, i.e., a bronc rider.

All the old-time saddles were this way; Western, English and military.

If your feet are held back by the stirrups, your upper body weight will get ahead of your belt buckle and you are off on the next jump. To stay off the reins on a rearing horse and not pull it back over on yourself - the stirrups need to swing back so you can keep your feet right under you and keep your balance.

For the same reason in hard athletic riding you need that stirrup to move around freely with your lower leg so you always have your balance and your seat. This is one of the major keys in a good seat. You can't have good hands that won't, when riding hard, jerk or pull on the mouth if you don't have a good balanced seat. (Balancing yourself with your feet).

Removing the back and foward plugs is easy to do - you just have to go do it.

It may not totally cure your saddle and make it a good performance/stand-up saddle, but it is a step in the right direction.

Removing the plugs will help to a certain degree improve your posture on some saddles. If the stirrups are too far forward, the seat too deep and the plate sloped up too high in front, the change over would not be worth the effort.

If the low spot is too far back, moving the stirrups may not be worth moving because the back end of the saddle will always be overloaded.

START WITH THE
STAND-UP SEAT

Once you have developed the fundamentals of the balanced Stand-Up Seat and the necessary skills to go with it, then you can move on to varying your style for other disciplines. But first get to where you can really ride a horse first, that will make you so much better at whatever else you try.

**THE SADDLE IS
75% of the
STAND-UP SEAT**

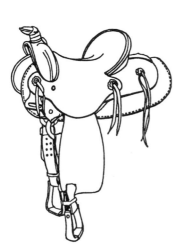

SUMMARY OF REQUIREMENTS FOR THE STAND-UP SEAT SADDLE:
The Stand-up Seat Western Saddle

75% of the Stand-Up Seat is the proper saddle.
The low point of the saddle is in the middle.
The top plate of the saddle is fairly flat.
The back half of the seat is fairly flat.
The front half has a fairly narrow crown.
The stirrups are no more than 4 to 5 inches ahead of the
  lowest point in the seat.
The stirrups are no more than half your width through your
  belt line ahead of the low point in the saddle.
The stirrups are free swinging: forward and back.
The curve around of the cantle is not so great as to cut
  into the back of your legs.
The cantle has a good 'cupping' effect.
The bars are about 2 inches shorter than the distance from
  the scapula hook to the last rib on the back.
The bars do not ride too high in front, this causes bridging
  between the withers and small of the back.
A good open channel down the back for cooling.
A good fit the whole length of the back.
The ends and edges are well rounded-up on the bars.
The horn or pommel does not sit too high. (forks). The horn
  can hit you in the stomach or get caught under your coat.
The saddle sits level and the plate sits level.
The stirrups do not ride up over the cinch 'D's.
The saddle bars extend a good 6 inches behind the cantle.
The saddle fits over the withers with room to spare with
  the blankets.
The skirts are all one piece of leather with no overlapping
  and they are fairly thick (3/8" to 7/16") and a little
  stiff.
Make sure the skirts and jockey in the back of the saddle
  curve up to help when horse flexes its back.

SUMMARY OF REQUIREMENTS FOR THE STAND-UP SEAT SADDLE:
The Stand-Up Seat English Saddle

Most English saddles are made for jumping and the stirrups are too far forward and the seat too far back. This makes them very hard to ride.

THE SADDLE IS 75% OF THE STAND-UP SEAT

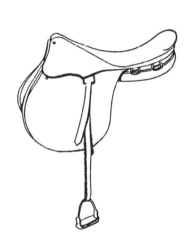

The saddle is 75% of the Stand-Up Seat.
The low point of the saddle is in the middle.
The stirrups are no more than 3 to 4 inches ahead of the lowest point of the seat.
The seat is fairly flat, not overly dished.
The back of the seat is flat - round seats are difficult to ride
The front half of the seat has a good crown.
The knee rolls do not make the saddle too wide.
The billets for the girth place the saddle 2" behind the scapula hook and do not go over the webbing of the front legs.
The rider's position should fall in the bareback crease just behind the withers in the lowest point on the back and the groove between the shoulders and the barrel.
The leather pads are a good 6 inches wide in back and 4 to 5 inches wide in front and fit the full length of the back, especially in the middle.
The saddle sits 2 inches behind the scapula hook to the last rib.
The throat is 2 inches, at least, over the withers and does not make saddle too high in front.
The saddle sits level with the pads and blankets on.
The throat has some flex or give to the throat.
The tree of the saddle is wide enough over the withers and is well padded.
The saddle is not made with tubing instead of flat bars.
It has a good air tunnel down the middle of the saddle.
The stirrup leathers are 1-1/4" wide and of good harness leather.
The spring loaded stirrup hangers are working.
The stirrup irons are a good 1-1/2 inches wider than your boot for easy exit.

BITS AND BITTING MANUAL
by William G. Langdon, Jr.

118 pages, 9 x 11, detailed illustrations, spiral bound. A How To Do It Manual. A users manual covering all the basic bits - what they can do and cannot do, what makes them work, and how to use them. How to train and use bits, martingales, draw-reins, hackamores, and understand what makes them work. Studies on all the major bits, leg aids, and reining techniques. Shows how bits are used in families and how to make bit selections. Every page is accompanied with helpful illustrations. The most complete bit book published.

TRAINING WITH BITS
by William G. Langdon, Jr.

106 pages, 9 x 11, detailed illustrations, spiral bound. A How To Do It Manual. A manual for the rider/trainer on how to use bits in sequence-training, stepping from bit to bit. Shows the reader how to select certain families of bits to match how the horse accepts the bit. Describes half stepping with bits, advancing the horse through a basic bit selection without losing "that nice snaffle training". Includes the Bitting Wall, which describes how to hang bits by their use characteristics, so one can know which bit to use next in training or solving problems. The text also includes a Bitting Chart that coincides with the Bitting Wall, but describes each bit and its fundamental use points. This is the follow-up text to "Bits and Bitting Manual" on HOW TO USE BITS. Many detailed illustrations. The only book on this subject ever published.

BITS, PATTERNS & REINING
by William G. Langdon, Jr.

166 pages, 9 x 11, detailed illustrations, spiral bound. A How To Do It Manual for the rider/trainer. A complete study relating the use of bits and patterns in teaching a horse to rein. Many past and present methods, in a step by step guide, for English or Western. A detailed outline of bits and patterns to use with each step of a progressive training program. Each step is detailed with helpful illustrations: colt training, basic training, secondary patterns, and finished maneuvers. From slides to spins, rollaways to rollins, 2-tracking and sidepassing, running turns, running backwards, lead changes, perfect circles, figure eights and balanced stops. Introduces the Wagon Wheel Pattern, which is fast and easy for the horse to understand and has them reining around in a short time. Also helps the horse with reining problems. If you like well reined horses you will like this manual. The most complete book published.

RIDE RIGHT
by William G. Langdon, Jr.

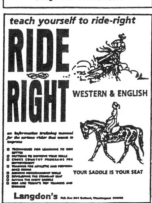

138 pages, 9 x 11, spiral bound, detailed instructions and a large supply of illustrations. This is a comprehensive manual for the serious rider who wants to improve their seat and riding skills. Instructions on selecting the proper saddle - because 75% of a good seat is the correct saddle. A step by step guide of specific exercises and techniques for improving your riding skills and the reader is bound only by their own ambitions and energy as to how far they wish to go in this program. If you want to ride like a winner, RIDE RIGHT is the manual to study.

LANGDON ENTERPRISES
P.O. Box 201 . Colbert, WA 99005